ALL LOVES EXCELLING

All Loves Excelling

The Saints' Knowledge of Christ's Love

JOHN BUNYAN

THE BANNER OF TRUTH TRUST

THE BANNER OF TRUTH TRUST
3 Murrayfield Road, Edinburgh EH12 6EL
P.O. Box 621, Carlisle, Pennsylvania 17013, USA

*

'The Saints' Knowledge of Christ's Love' first published 1692
First Banner of Truth edition 1998
© Banner of Truth 1998
ISBN 0 85151 739 0

Typeset in 10½/12pt Linotron Plantin
at The Spartan Press Ltd,
Lymington, Hants
and printed and bound in Finland by
WSOY

CONTENTS

'THAT YE . . . MAY BE ABLE TO COMPREHEND
WITH ALL SAINTS, WHAT *IS* THE BREADTH, AND
LENGTH, AND DEPTH, AND HEIGHT; AND TO
KNOW THE LOVE OF CHRIST, WHICH PASSETH
KNOWLEDGE.'—EPH. 3: 18, 19.

PUBLISHERS' FOREWORD

This is a new edition of John Bunyan's treatise on Ephesians 3:17b–19 which he himself prepared for the press. It is taken from the second volume of Bunyan's works (George Offor edition) which was re-published by the Trust in 1991. The text remains largely unaltered but slight adjustments have been made in order to accommodate the arrangement of the material into chapters. Even these divisions, however, correspond to Bunyan's own layout of his material. A detailed breakdown of the structure of Bunyan's meditation on the greatness of the love of Christ is found at the end of this book by way of an appendix.

This subject matter of this work which was first preached, is greatly needed today. On the one hand, experiences of the Spirit are being claimed from which the glory of the redeemer and the wonder of his love are quite absent, while on the other, an almost total attention to the understanding and practising of scripture truth is having the effect of marginalising the experiential element in true, spiritual knowledge.

Bunyan's description of Christ's love to believers and how they ought to know it, cuts in both the above-mentioned directions. From some 440 Bible references he shows how knowing Christ's love is the message of Scripture and also the essence of heaven, partly possessed and expressed on earth. Those who know it are rich beyond measure and they are the people who 'sweeten the churches and bring glory to God and to religion'.

PART ONE

Describing the Inexpressible

1: *Ephesians 3:18, 19 in Context*

The Apostle having, in the first chapter, treated the doctrine of election, and in the second, of the reconciling of the Gentiles with the Jews to the Father, by his Son, through the preaching of the gospel; comes in the third chapter to show that *that* also was, as that of election, determined before the world began. Now lest the afflictions that attend the gospel should, by its raging among these Ephesians, darken the glory of these things unto them; therefore he makes here a brief repetition and explanation, to the end they might be supported and made live above them. He also joins thereto a fervent prayer for them, that God would let them see in the spirit and faith, how they, by God and by Christ, are secured from the evil of the worst that might come upon them. 'For this cause I bow my knees unto the Father of our Lord Jesus Christ, of whom the whole family in heaven and earth is named; that he would grant you, according to the riches of his glory, to be strengthened with might by his Spirit in the inner man; that Christ may dwell in your hearts by faith; and ye, being rooted and grounded in love, may be able to comprehend with all saints, what *is* the breadth, and length, and depth, and height; and to know the love of Christ, which passeth knowledge,' &c. Knowing, that their deep understanding what good by these were reserved for them, they would never be discouraged, whatever troubles should attend their profession.

(I) THE TERMS OF MEASUREMENT

BREADTH, and LENGTH, and DEPTH, and HEIGHT, are words that in themselves are both ambiguous, and to wonderment; ambiguous, because unexplained, and to wonderment, because they carry in them an unexpressible something; and *that* something that which far out-goes all those things that can be found in this world. The Apostle here was under a spiritual surprise, for while meditating and writing, he was caught: The strength and glory of the truths that he was endeavouring to fasten upon the people to whom he wrote, took him away into their glory, beyond what could to the full be uttered. Besides, many times things are thus expressed, on purpose to command attention, a stop and pause in the mind about them; and to divert, by their greatness, the heart from the world, unto which they naturally are so inclined. Also, truths are often delivered to us, like wheat in full ears, to the end we should rub them out before we eat them, and take pains *about* them, before we have the comfort of them.

BREADTH, LENGTH, DEPTH, and HEIGHT. In my attempting to open these words, I will give you, some that are of the same kind. And then show you, First, The reasons of them; and then also, Secondly, Something of their fulness.

Those of the same kind, are used sometimes to shew us the power, force, and subtlety of the enemies of God's church (*Dan.* 4:11, *Rom.* 8:38, 39). But,

[*Sometimes*] Most properly to shew us the infinite and unsearchable greatness of God (*Job* 11:7, 8, 9. *Rom.* 11:33).

They are here to be taken in this second sense, that is, to suggest unto us the unsearchable and infinite greatness of God; who is a *breadth*, beyond all breadths; a *length*, beyond all lengths; a *depth*, beyond all depths; and a

[4]

height, beyond all heights, and that in all his attributes: He is an eternal being, an everlasting being, and in that respect he is beyond all measures, whether they be of breadth, or length, or depth, or height. In all his attributes he is beyond all measure: whether you measure by words, by thoughts, or by the most enlarged and exquisite apprehension; His greatness is unsearchable; His judgments are unsearchable (*Job* 5:9). He is infinite in wisdom. 'O! the depth of the riches both of the wisdom and knowledge of God!' (*Rom.* 11:33). 'If I speak of strength, lo, he is strong;' (*Job* 9:19); yea, 'the thunder of his power who can understand?' (*Job* 26:14). 'There is none holy as the Lord:' (*1 Sam.* 2:2), 'and his mercy is from everlasting to everlasting, upon them that fear him.' (*Psa.* 103:17). The *greatness* of God, of the God and Father of our Lord Jesus Christ, is that, if rightly considered, which will support the spirits of those of his people that are frighted with the greatness of their adversaries. For here is a greatness against a greatness. Pharaoh was great, but God more great, more great in power, more great in wisdom, more great every way for the help of his people; wherein they dealt proudly, he was above them. These words therefore take in for this people, the great God who in his immensity and infinite greatness is beyond all beings.

(II) THE REASON FOR THEIR USE

They are made use of to show to the Ephesians, that God with what he is in himself, and with what he hath in his power, is all for the use and profit of the believers. Else no great matter is held out to them thereby. 'But this God is our God!' there is the comfort: For this cause therefore he presenteth them with this description of him. To wit, by breadth, and length, and depth, and height: As who

[5]

should say, the High God is yours; the God that fills heaven and earth is yours; the God whom the heaven of heavens cannot contain, is yours; yea, the God whose works are wonderful, and whose ways are past finding out, is yours. Consider therefore the greatness that is for you, that taketh part with you, and that will always come in for your help against them that contend with you. It is my support, it is my relief; it [is] my comfort in all my tribulations, and I would have it yours, and so it will when we live in the lively faith thereof. Nor should we admit of distrust in this matter from the consideration of our own unworthiness, either taken from the finiteness of our state, or the foulness of our ways (*Psa.* 46). For now, though God's attributes, several of them in their own nature, are set against sin and sinners; yea, were we righteous, are so high that needs they must look over us, for 'tis to him a condescension to behold things in heaven: How much more then to open his eyes upon such as we: yet by the passion of Jesus Christ, they harmoniously agree in the salvation of our souls. Hence God is said to be *love* (*1 John* 4). God is *love*; might some say, and *justice* too: but his justice is turned with wisdom, power, holiness and truth, to love; yea, to love those that be found in his Son: forasmuch as there is nothing fault-worthy in his righteousness which is put upon us. So then, as there is in God's nature a *length*, and *breadth* and *depth*, and *height*, that is beyond all that we can think: So we should conclude that all this is *love* to us, for Christ's sake; and then dilate with it thus in our minds, and enlarge it thus in our meditations; saying still to our low and trembling spirits: 'It is high as heaven; what canst thou do? deeper than hell; what canst thou know? the measure thereof *is* longer than the earth, and broader than the sea.' (*Job* 11:8, 9)

[6]

(III) THE FULNESS IMPLIED IN THEM

But we will pass generals, and more particularly speak *of their fulness*, as they are fitted to suit and answer to the whole state and condition of a Christian in this life. The words are boundless; we have here a breadth, a length, a depth, and height made mention of; but *what* breadth, *what* length, *what* depth, *what* height is not so much as hinted. It is therefore infiniteness suggested to us, and that has engaged for us. For the Apostle conjoins therewith, *And to know the love of Christ which passeth knowledge.* Thus therefore it suits and answers a Christian's condition, while in this world, let that be what it will. If his afflictions be broad, here is a breadth; if they be long, here is a length; and if they be deep, here is a depth; and if they be high, here is a height. And I will say, there is nothing that is more helpful, succouring, or comfortable to a Christian while in a state of trial and temptation, than to know that there is a *breadth* to answer a breadth, a *length* to answer a length, a *depth* to answer a depth, and a *height* to answer a height. Wherefore this is it that the Apostle prayeth for, namely, that the Ephesians might have understanding in these things, 'That ye may know what is the breadth, and length, and depth, and height.'

Of the largeness of the Apostle's heart in praying for this people, to wit, 'That they might be able to comprehend with all saints, what,' &c. of that we shall speak afterwards. But first, to speak to these four expressions, breadth, length, depth, and height.

2: *The Breadth of Christ's Love*

This word BREADTH is to show, that God is all over, everywhere, spreading of his wings, stretching out his goodness to the *utmost bounds*, for the good of those that are his people (*Deut.* 32:11, 12; *Gen.* 49:26).

In the sin of his people there is a *breadth*; a breadth that spreadeth *over all*, wheresoever a man shall look. The sin of the saints is a spreading leprosy (*Lev.* 13:12). Sin is a scab that spreadeth; it is a spreading plague; it knows no bounds (*Lev.* 13:8, 57) or, as David saith, 'I have seen the wicked spreading himself' (*Psa.* 37:35). Hence it is compared to a cloud, to a thick cloud, that covereth or spreadeth over the face of all the sky. Wherefore here is a breadth called for, a *breadth* that can cover all, or else what is done is to no purpose. Therefore to answer this, here we have a *breadth*, a spreading breadth; 'I spread my skirt over thee:' But how far? Even so far as to cover all. 'I spread my skirt over thee, and covered thy nakedness' (*Ezek.* 16:8). Here now is a breadth according to the spreading nature of the sin of this wretched one; yea, a super-abounding spreading; a spreading *beyond*; a spreading to cover. 'Blessed *is he whose* sin *is* covered' (*Psa.* 32:1), whose spreading sin is covered by the mercy of God through Christ (*Rom.* 4:4–7). This is the spreading cloud, whose spreadings none can understand (*Job* 36:29). 'He spread a cloud for a covering, and fire to give light in the night' (*Psa.* 105:39).

This breadth that is in God, it also overmatcheth that

spreading and overspreading rage of men, that is sometimes as if it would swallow up the whole church of God. You read of the rage of the king of Assyria, that there was a *breadth* in it, an *overflowing* breadth, to the filling of 'the breadth of thy land, O Immanuel' (*Isa.* 8:8). But what follows? 'Associate yourselves, O ye people, (ye Assyrians) and ye shall be broken in pieces; and give ear, all ye of far countries; gird yourselves and ye shall be broken in pieces. Take counsel together, and it shall come to nought; speak the word, and it shall not stand, for God is with us' (*Isa.* 8:8–10). God will over-match and go beyond you.

Wherefore this word, *breadth, and what is the breadth*: It is here expressed on purpose to succour and relieve, or to show what advantage, for support, the knowledge of the overspreading grace of God by Christ yieldeth unto those that have it, let their trials be what they will. Alas! the sin of God's children seemeth sometimes to overspread not only their flesh, and the face of their souls, but the whole face of heaven. And what shall he do now, that is a stranger to *this breadth*, made mention of in the text? Why he must despair, lie down and die, and shut up his heart against all comfort, unless he, with his fellow-Christians, can, at least, apprehend what is *this* breadth, or the breadth of mercy intended in this place. Therefore Paul for the support of the Ephesians, prays, that they may know 'what is the breadth.'

This largeness of the heart and mercy of God towards his people, is also signified by the *spreading* out of his hand to us in the invitations of the gospel. 'I said,' saith he, 'Behold me, behold me, . . . I have spread out my hands all the day unto a rebellious people, . . . to a people that provoketh me continually' (*Isa.* 65:1–3).

I have spread out my hands, that is, opened my arms as a mother affectionately doth, when she stoopeth to her

[9]

child in the warm workings of her bowels, and claspeth it up in them, and kisseth, and putteth it into her bosom.

For, by spreading out the hands or arms to embrace, is showed the breadth or largeness of God's affections; as by our spreading out our hands in prayer, is signified the great sense that we have of the spreading nature of our sins, and of the great desires that are in us, that God would be merciful to us (*Ezra* 9:5–7).

This word also answereth to, or may fitly be set against the wiles and temptations of the devil, who is that great and dogged Leviathan, that spreadeth his 'sharp-pointed things upon the mire' (*Job* 41:30). For, be the spreading nature of our corruptions never so broad, he will find sharp-pointed things enough to stick in the mire *of them*, for our affliction. These sharp-pointed things are those that in another place are called 'fiery darts' (*Eph.* 6:16), and he has abundance of them, with which he can and will sorely prick and wound our spirits: Yea, so sharp some have found these things to their souls, that they have pierced beyond expression. 'When,' said Job, 'I say, my bed shall comfort me, my couch shall ease my complaint; then thou scarest me with dreams, and terrifiest me through visions; so that my soul chooseth strangling, *and* death rather than my life' (*Job* 7:13–15). But now, answerable to the spreading of these sharp-pointed things, there is a super-abounding breadth in the sovereign grace of God, the which whoso seeth and understandeth, as the Apostle doth pray we should, is presently helped: for he seeth that this grace spreadeth itself, and is broader than can be, either our mire, or the sharp-pointed things that he spreadeth thereupon for our vexation and affliction: 'It is broader than the sea' (*Job* 11:9).

This therefore should be that upon which those that see the spreading nature of sin, and the leprosy and contagion thereof, should meditate, to wit, The *broadness* of the grace and mercy of God in Christ. This will poise and stay the soul; this will relieve and support the soul in and under those many misgiving and desponding thoughts unto which we are subject when afflicted with the apprehensions of sin, and the abounding nature of it.

Shall *another* man pray for this, one that knew the goodness and benefit of it, and shall not I meditate upon it? and shall not I exercise my mind about it? Yes, surely, for it is *my* duty, it is *my* privilege and mercy so to do. Let this therefore, when thou seest the spreading nature of thy sin be a *memento* to thee, to the end thou may'st not sink and die in thy soul.

3: *The Length of Christ's Love*

What is the breadth and LENGTH. As there is a *breadth* in this mercy and grace of God by Christ, so there is a LENGTH therein, and this *length* is as *large* as the *breadth*, and as much suiting the condition of the child of God, as the other is. For, though sin sometimes is most afflicting to the conscience, while the soul beholdeth the over-spreading nature of it, yet here it stoppeth not, but oft-times through the power and prevalency of it, the soul is driven with it, as a ship by a mighty tempest, or as a rolling thing before the whirlwind: driven, I say, from God, and from all hopes of his mercy, *as far* as the east is from the west, or as the ends of the world are asunder. Hence it is supposed by the prophet, that for and by sin they may be driven from God to the utmost part of heaven (*Deut.* 30:4); and that is a sad thing, a sad thing, I say, to a gracious man. 'Why,' saith the prophet to God, 'Art thou so far from helping me, and from the words of my roaring?' (*Psa.* 22:1). Sometimes a man, yea, a man of God, is, as he apprehends, so *far* off from God, that he can neither *help* him, nor *hear* him, and this is a dismal state. 'And thou hast removed my soul,' said the church, 'far off from peace: I forgat prosperity' (*Lam.* 3:17). This is the state sometimes of the godly, and that not only with reference to their being removed by persecutors, from the ap-pointments and gospel-seasons, which are their delight, and the desire of their eyes; but also with reference to their faith and hope in their God. They think themselves beyond the reach of his mercy. Wherefore in answer to this conceit it is, that the Lord asketh, saying, 'Is my hand shortened at all that it cannot redeem?' (*Isa.* 50:2). And again, 'Behold, the Lord's hand is not shortened, that it cannot save; neither his ear heavy, that it cannot hear' (*Isa.* 59:1). Wherefore he saith again, 'If any of them be driven out unto the outmost parts of heaven, from thence will the Lord thy God gather thee, and from thence will he fetch thee' (*Deut.* 30:4). God has a *long* arm, and he can *reach* a great way further than we can conceive he can (*Neh.* 1:9).

When we think his mercy is *clean* gone, and that ourselves are *free* among the dead, and of the number that he remembereth no more, *then* he can reach us, and cause that again we stand before him. He *could* reach Jonah, tho' in the belly of hell (*Jon.* 2); and reach thee, even then, when thou thinkest thy way is hid from the Lord, and thy judgment passed over from thy God. There is a *length* to admiration, beyond apprehension or belief, in the arm of the strength of the Lord; and this is that which the Apostle intended by this word, *Length*; namely, To insinuate what a *reach* there is in the mercy of God, how *far* it can extend itself. 'If I take the wings of the morning,' said David, 'and dwell in the uttermost parts of the sea; even there shall thy hand lead me, and thy right hand shall hold me' (*Psa.* 139:9, 10). I will gather them from the east, and from the west, and from the north, and from the south, saith he: That is, from the utmost corners.

This therefore should encourage them that for the present cannot stand, but that do fly before their guilt: Them that feel no help nor stay, but that go, as to their thinking, every day by the power of temptation, driven yet farther off from God, and from the hope of obtaining of his mercy to their salvation; poor creature, I will not now ask thee how thou camest into this condition, or how long this has been thy state; but I will say before thee, and I prithee hear me, *O the length of the saving arm of God!* As yet thou art within the reach thereof; do not thou go about to measure arms with God, as some good men are apt to do: I mean, do not thou conclude, that because thou canst not reach God by thy short stump, therefore he cannot reach thee with his long arm. Look again, 'Hast thou an arm like God' (*Job* 40:9), an arm like his for length and strength? It becomes thee, when thou canst not perceive that God is within the reach of *thy* arm, then to believe that thou art within the reach of *his*; for it is long, and none knows how long.

Again, is there such a *length*? *such* a length in the arm of the Lord, that he can reach those that are gone away, as far as they could? then this should encourage us to pray, and hope for the salvation of any one of our backslidden relations, that God would reach out his arm after them: Saying, 'Awake, . . . O arm of the Lord, – art thou not it that hath cut Rahab, *and* wounded the dragon? *Art* thou not it which hath dried the sea, the waters of the great deep, that hath made the depths of the sea a way for the ransomed to pass over?' (*Isa.* 51:9, 10). Awake, O arm of the Lord, and be stretched out as far as to where my poor husband is, where my poor child, or to where my poor backslidden wife or dear relation is, and lay hold, fast hold; they are gone from thee, but, O thou the hope of Israel, fetch them again, and let them stand before thee. I say, here is in this word LENGTH matter of encouragement for us thus to pray; for if the length of the reach of mercy is *so great*, and if also this length is for the benefit of those that may be gone off *far* from God, (for they at present have no need thereof that are near) then improve this advantage at the throne of grace for such, that they may come to God again.

4: *The Depth of Christ's Love*

As there is a *breadth* and *length* here, so there is a DEPTH. What is the breadth, and length, and depth? And this depth is also put in here, on purpose to help us under a trial that is diverse from the two former. I told you, that by the *breadth* the apostle insinuates a remedy and succour to us, when we see our corruptions spread like a leprosy; and by *length* he would shew us, that when sin has driven God's elect to the farthest distance from him, yet his arm is long enough to reach them, and fetch them back again.

But, I say, as we have here a *breadth*, and a *length*, so we have also a *depth*. That ye may know what is the DEPTH. Christians have sometimes their sinking fits, and are as if they were always descending: or as Heman says, 'counted with them that go down into the pit' (*Psa.* 88:4). Now guilt is not to such so much a wind and a tempest, as a load and burden. The *devil*, and *sin*, and the *curse* of the law, and *death*, are gotten upon the shoulders of this poor man, and are treading of him down, that he may sink into, and be swallowed up of *his* miry place.

'I sink,' says David, 'in deep mire, where there is no standing. I am come into DEEP waters, where the floods overflow me' (*Psa.* 69:2). Yea, there is nothing more common among the saints of old, than this complaint: 'Let neither the water flood overflow me, neither let the deep swallow me up, neither let the pit shut her mouth upon me' (*Psa.* 69:14, 15). Heman also saith, 'Thou hast laid me in the lowest pit, in darkness, in the deeps. Thy wrath lieth hard upon me, and thou hast afflicted me with all thy waves' (*Psa.* 88:6, 7). Hence it is again that the Psalmist says: 'Deep calleth unto deep, at the noise of thy water spouts: all thy waves, and thy billows are gone over me' (*Psa.* 42:7). *Deep* calleth unto *deep*: What's that? Why, it is expressed in the verse before: 'O God,' says he, 'My soul is cast down within me.' 'Down,' that is, *deep* into the jaws of distrust and fear. And, Lord, my soul in this *depth* of sorrow calls for help to thy *depth* of mercy. For though I am sinking and going down, yet not so low, but that thy mercy is yet underneath me: Do of thy compassions open those everlasting arms (*Deut.* 33:27), and catch him that has no help or stay in himself: For so it is with one that is falling into a *well* or a *dungeon*.

Now mark, as there is in these texts, the sinking condition of the godly may set forth, of a man whom sin and Satan is treading down into the *deep*; so in our text which I am speaking to at this time, we have a *depth* that can more than counterpoise these *deeps*, set forth with a hearty prayer, that we may know it. And although the deeps, or depths of calamity into which the godly may fall, may be as *deep* as Hell, and methinks they should be no deeper: yet *this* is the comfort, and for the comfort of them of the godly that are thus a sinking: The mercy of God for them lies *deeper*. 'It is deeper than hell, what canst thou know?' (*Job* 11:8). And this is that which made Paul that he was not afraid of this *depth*, 'I am persuaded,' saith he, 'that neither . . . height nor depth shall be able to separate us from the love of God, which is in Christ Jesus our Lord' (*Rom.* 8:38, 39). But of this he could by no means have been persuaded, had he not believed that mercy lieth deeper for the godly to help them, than can all other depths be to destroy them: This is it at which he stands and wonders, saying, 'O the depth of the riches both of the wisdom and knowledge of God' (*Rom.* 11:33), that is to find out a way to save his people, notwithstanding all the deep contrivances that the enemy hath, and may invent to make us come short [of] home.

This is also that, as I take it, which is wrapped up in the blessing, wherewith Jacob blessed his son Joseph. 'God shall bless thee,' saith he, 'with blessings of heaven above,' and with the 'blessings of the deep that lieth under' (*Gen.* 49:25). A blessing which he had ground to pronounce, as well from his observation of God's good dealing with Joseph, as in a spirit of prophecy: For he saw that he lived and was become a flourishing bough, by a wall, after that the archers had done their worst to him (*Gen.* 49:22–24). Moses also blesseth God for blessing of Joseph thus, and blessed his portion to him, as counting of it sufficient for his help in all afflictions. 'Blessed,' saith he, 'of the Lord, be his land, for the precious things of heaven, for the dew, and for the deep that coucheth beneath' (*Deut.* 33:13).

I am not of belief that these blessings are confined to things temporal, or carnal, but to things spiritual and divine; and that they have most chiefly respect to soul, and eternal good. Now mark, he tells us here, that the blessings of the *deep*, do *couch* beneath. *Couch*, that is, lie close, so as hardly to be discerned by him that willingly would see that himself is not below these arms that are beneath him. But that as I said, is hard to be discerned by him that thus is sinking, and that has as he now smartingly feels, all God's waves, and his billows rolling over him. However, whether he sees or not, for this blessing lieth *couched*; yet there it is, and there will be, though one should sink as deep as hell: And hence they are said to be 'everlasting arms' that are 'underneath' (*Deut.* 33:27). That is, arms that are *long* and *strong*, and that can reach to the bottom, and also beyond, of all misery and distress, that Christians are subject to in this life. Indeed mercy

[17]

seems to be asleep, when we are sinking: for then we are as if all things were careless of us, but it is but as a *lion couchant*, it will awake in time for our help (*Psa.* 44:22, 26; *Mark* 4:36–39). And forasmuch as this term is it, which is applicable to the lion in his den; it may be to shew that as a lion, so will God at the fittest season, arise for the help and deliverance of a sinking people. Hence when he is said to address himself to the delivering of his people, it is that he comes as a roaring lion. 'The Lord shall go forth as a mighty man, he shall stir up jealousy like a man of war: he shall cry, yea, roar; he shall prevail against his enemies' (*Isa.* 42:13). However here is a depth against the depth that's against us, let *that* depth be what it will. As let it be the depth of misery, the depth of mercy is sufficient. If it be the depth of hellish policy, the depth both of the wisdom and knowledge of God shall go beyond it, and prevail.

This therefore is worthy of the consideration of all sinking souls; of the souls that feel themselves descending into the pit. There is such a thing as this experienced among the godly. Come to them (when tempted) when you will, they will tell you, they have no ground to stand on, their feet have slipped, their foundation is removed, and they feel themselves sinking, as into a pit that has no bottom (*Psa.* 11:3). They inwardly sink, not for want of something to relieve the body, but for want of some spiritual cordial to support the mind. 'I went down to the bottoms of the mountains,' said Jonas, 'the earth with her bars *was* about me for ever; . . . my soul fainted within me' (*Jon.* 2:6, 7).

Now for such to consider that *underneath* them, even at the *bottom* there lieth a blessing, or that in this deep whereinto they are descending, there lieth a delivering mercy couching to catch them, and to save them from sinking for ever, this would be relief unto them, and help them to hope for good.

Again, As this, were it well considered by the sinking ones, would yield them stay and relief, so this is it by the virtue whereof, they that have been sinking heretofore, have been lifted up, and above their castings down again. There are of those that have been in the *pit*, now upon mount *Sion*, with the harps of God in their hands, and with the song of the Lamb in their mouths. But how is it that they are there? why, David, by his own deliverance shows you the reason. 'For great is thy mercy towards me,' saith he, 'and thou hast delivered my soul from the lowest hell' (*Psa.* 86:13). And again, 'He brought me up also out of an horrible pit,' (a pit of noise, a pit wherein was the noise of devils, and of my heart answering them with distrust and fear) 'out of the miry clay,' (into which I did not only sink, but was by it held from getting up: but he brought me up) 'and set my feet upon a rock, and established my goings. And he hath put a new song in my mouth, even praise to our God' (*Psa.* 40:2, 3).

But let me here give, if it may be, a timely caution to them that think they stand upon their feet. Give not way to falling because everlasting arms are underneath, take heed of that: God can let thee fall into mischief, he can let thee fall, and not help thee up. Tempt not God, lest he cast thee away indeed. I doubt there are many that have presumed upon this mercy, that thus do couch beneath, and have cast themselves down from their pinnacles into vanity, of a vain conceit that they shall be lifted up again: whom yet God will leave to die there, because their fall was rather of *willfulness*, than *weakness*, and of stubbornness, and desperate resolutions, than for want of means and helps to preserve them from it.

5: *The Height of Christ's Love*

As there is a *breadth*, and *length*, and *depth*, in this mercy and grace of God through Christ towards his people: So there is also a HEIGHT, 'That ye may comprehend with all saints, what is the breadth and length, and depth, and HEIGHT.' There are things that are *high*, as well as things that are *low*; things that are *above* us, as well as things that are *under*, that are distressing to God's people. It is said when Noah was a preacher of righteousness, there were *giants* in the earth in those days (*Gen.* 6:4). And these, as I conceive, were some of the heights that were set against Noah; yea, they were the very *dads* and fathers of all that monstrous brood that followed in the world in that day. Of this sort were they who so frighted, and terrified Israel, when they were to go to inherit the land of promise. The men that were *tall* as the cedars, and *strong* as the oaks, frighted them: they were in their own sight, when compared with these high ones, but as grasshoppers. This therefore was their discouragement (*Num.* 13:31–33; *Deut.* 2:10; 9:2).

Besides, together with these, they had *high walls*, walls as high as heaven; and these walls were of purpose to keep Israel out of his possession. See how it is expressed: The people is greater and taller than we, the cities are great and walled up to heaven: and moreover, we have seen the sons of the Anakims there (*Deut.* 1:28). One of these, to wit, Goliath by name, how did he fright the children of Israel in the days of Saul! How did the appearance of him, make them scuttle together on heaps before him (*1 Sam.* 17). By these *giants*, and by these *high walls*, God's children to this day are sorely distressed, because they stand in the cross ways to cut off Israel from his possession.

But now to support us against all these, and to encourage us to take heart notwithstanding all these things; there is for us, a height in God. He hath made his Son higher than the kings of the earth (*Psa.* 89:26, 28). His word also is settled for ever in heaven, and therefore must needs be higher than their walls (*Psa.* 119:89). He also saith in another place, 'If thou seest the oppression of the poor, and violent perverting of judgment and justice in a province, marvel not at the matter; for he that is higher than the highest, regardeth, and there be higher than they' (*Eccles.* 5.8). 'Twas this that made Paul, that he feared not the height: not things present, nor things to come (*Rom.* 8:39).

But again, As there are these things standing, or lying in our way: So there are another sort of heights that are more mischievous than these: And they are the fallen angels. These are called spiritual wickedness, *or wicked spirits*, in high places (*Eph.* 6:12). For God has suffered them for a time to take to themselves principality and power, and so they are become the rulers of the darkness of this world. By these we are tempted, sifted, threatened, opposed, undermined: also by these there are snares, pits, holes, and what not made and laid for us, if peradventure by something we may be destroyed. Yea, and we should most certainly be so, were it not for the rock that is *higher* than they. 'But he that cometh from heaven is above all!' (*John* 3:31). These are they that our king has taken captive, and hath rid (in his chariots of salvation) in triumph over their necks. These are they, together with all others, whose most devilish designs he can wield, and turn and make work together for his ransomed's advantage (*Rom.* 8:28).

There is a height, an infinitely overtopping height in the mercy and goodness of God for us, against them.

There are heights also that build up themselves *in* us, which are not but to be taken notice of: Yea, there are a *many* of them, and they place themselves directly so, that if possible they may keep the saving knowledge of God out of our hearts. These high things therefore are said to exalt themselves against the knowledge of God (*2 Cor.* 10:5); and do offtimes more plague, afflict, and frighten Christian men and women, than any thing besides. It is from these that our faith and spiritual understanding of God, and his Christ is opposed and contradicted; and from these also that we are so inclinable to swerve from right doctrine into destructive opinions. 'Tis from these that we are so easily persuaded to call into question our former experience of the goodness of God towards us, and from these that our minds are so often clouded and darkened that we cannot see afar off. These would betray us into the hands of fallen angels, and men, nor should we by any means help or deliver ourselves, were it not for one that is higher. These are the dark mountains at which our feet would certainly stumble, and upon which we should fall, were it not for one who can *leap* and *skip* over these mountains of division, and come in to us (*Song of Sol.* 2:8, 17).

Further, There is a height also that is obvious to our senses, the which when it is dealt withal by our corrupted reason, proves a great shaking to our mind, and that is the height, and exceeding distance that heaven is off of us, and we off it. 'Is not God in the height of heaven? and behold the height of the stars, how high they are?' (*Job* 22:12). Hence heaven is called the place for height (*Prov.* 25:3). Also when Ahaz is bid to ask with reference to heaven, he is bid to ask it, In the height, the height above (*Isa.* 7:11). Now saith reason, how shall I come thither? especially when a good man is at his furthest distance therefrom: which is, when he is in the grave. Now I say, every height is a difficulty to him that is laden with a burden, especially the heaven of heavens, where God is, and where is the resting-place of his, to them that are oppressed with the guilt of sin. And besides, the dispensation which happeneth to us last, to wit, death, as I said before, makes this heaven, in my thoughts while I live so much the more unaccessible. Christ indeed could mount up (*Acts* 1:9), but *me, poor me*, how shall I get thither? Elias indeed had a chariot sent him to ride in thither, and went up by it into that holy place (*2 Kings* 2:11), but I, poor I, how shall I get thither? Enoch is there, because God took him (*Gen.* 5.24): but, as for *me* how shall I get thither? Thus some have mourningly said. And although distrust of the power of God, as to the accomplishing of this thing, is by no means to be smiled upon, yet methinks the unconcernedness of professors thereabout, doth argue that considering thoughts about that, are wanting.

I know the answer is ready. *Get Christ and go to heaven.* But methinks the height of the place, and the glory of the state that we are to enjoy therein, should a little concern us, at least so as to make us wonder in our thinking, that the time is coming that we must mount up thither. And since there are so many heights between *this* place, between us, and *that*; it should make us admire at the heights of the grace and mercy of God, by which, means is provided to bring us thither. And I believe that this thing, this very thing, is included here by the Apostle when he prays for the Ephesians, that they might know the height.

Methinks, *How shall we get thither* will still stick in my mind. 'I will ascend,' says one, 'above the height of the clouds, I will be like the most High' (*Isa.* 14:14). And I, says another, will set my nest among the stars of heaven (*Obad.* 4). Well, but what of all this? If heaven has gates,

[23]

and they shall be shut, how wilt thou go in thither? Though such should climb up to heaven, from thence will God bring them down (*Amos* 9:2). Still I say, therefore, how shall we get in thither? Why, for them that are godly, there is the power of God, the merits of Christ, the help of angels, and the testimony of a good conscience to bring them thither; and he that has not the help of all these, let him do what he can, shall never come thither. Not that all these go to the making up of the height that is intended in the text: for the height there, is what is in God through Christ to us alone. But the angels are the servants of God for that end (*Luke* 16:32; *Heb.* 1:14) and none with ill consciences enter in thither (*Psa.* 15:1; 24:3, 4). What, 'know ye not that the unrighteous shall not inherit the kingdom of God? be not deceived' (*1 Cor.* 6:9), such have none inheritance in the kingdom of Christ and of God (*Eph.* 5.5).

This then should teach us that in God is a power that is able to subdue all things to himself. In the completing of many things, there seems to be an utter impossibility, as that a virgin should conceive in her womb, as a virgin, and bring a Son into the world; that the body that is turned into dust, should arise and ascend into the highest heaven (*Phil.* 3:21). These things with many more seem to be utterly impossible: but there is that which is called the power of God, by the which he is able to make all things bend to his will, and to make all obstructions give place to what he pleases. God is high above all things and can do whatever it pleaseth him. But since he can do so, why doth he suffer this, and that thing to appear, to act, and do so horribly repugnant to his word? I answer, he admits of many things, to the end he may show his wrath, and make his power known; and that all the world may see how he checks and overrules the most vile and unruly things, and can make them subservient to his holy will. And how would the *breadth* and the *length*, and the *depth*, and the *height* of the love and mercy of God in Christ to us-ward, be made to appear, so as in all things it doth, were there not admitted that there should be *breadths*, and *lengths*, and *depths* and *heights*, to oppose. Wherefore these oppositions are therefore suffered, that the greatness of the wisdom, the power, the mercy, and grace of God to us in Christ might appear and be made manifest unto us.

This calls therefore upon Christians, wisely to consider the doings of their God. How many opposite breadths, and lengths, and depths, and heights did Israel meet with in their journey from Egypt to Canaan, and all to convince them of their own weakness, and also of the power of their God. And they that did wisely consider of his doings there, did reap the advantage thereof. Come, behold the works of the Lord towards me, may every Christian say. He hath set a Saviour against sin; a heaven against a hell; light against darkness; good against evil, and the *breadth*, and *length*, and *depth*, and *height* of the grace that is in himself, for my good, against all the power, and strength, and force, and subtlety, of every enemy.

This also, as I hinted but just before, shows both the power of them that hate us, and the inability of us to resist. The power that is set against us none can crush, and break, but God: for it is the power of devils, of sin, of death, and hell. But we for our parts are crushed before the moth: being a shadow, a vapour, and a wind that passes away (*Job* 4:19). Oh! how should we, and how would we, were but our eyes awake, stand and wonder at the preservations, the deliverances, the salvations and benefits with which we are surrounded daily: while so many mighty evils seek daily to swallow us up, as the grave. See how the golden psalm of David reads it. 'Be merciful unto me, O God; for man would swallow me up; he fighting daily oppresseth me. Mine enemies would

[25]

daily swallow me up: for they be many that fight against me, O thou most high' (*Psa.* 56:1, 2). This is at the beginning of it. And he concludes it thus, 'Thou hast delivered my soul from death: wilt not thou deliver my feet from falling, that I may walk before God in the light of the living' (verse 13).

By this also we see the reason why it is so impossible for man or angel to persuade unbelievers to come in to, and close *with* Christ; why there is a *breadth* that they cannot get over, a *length* that they cannot get beyond, a *depth* that they cannot pass, and *heights* that so hinder them of the prospect of glory, and the way thereto, that they cannot be allured thither. And that nothing can remove these; but *those* that are in God, and that are opposite thereto; even the *breadth*, and *length*, and *depth* and *height* that is in the text expressed, is to all awakened men an undoubted truth.

One item I would here give to him that loveth his own soul, and then we will pass on in pursuance of what is to come. Since there is an height obvious to sense, and that that height must be overcome ere a man can enter into life eternal: let thy heart be careful that thou go the right way to overpass this height, that thou mayest not miss of the delectable plains, and the pleasures that are above. Now, there is nothing so *high*, as to overtop this *height*; but Jacob's ladder, and that can do it: that ladder, when the foot thereof doth stand upon the earth, reacheth with its top to the gate of heaven. This is the ladder by which angels ascend thither: and this is the ladder by which thou mayest ascend thither. 'And he dreamed, and behold a ladder set up on the earth, and the top of it reached to heaven: and behold the angels of God ascending and descending on it' (*Gen.* 28:12).

This ladder is Jesus Christ, the son of man, as is clear by the evangelist John (*John* 1:51). And in that it is said to stand upon the earth, that is to show that he took hold of man who is of the earth, and therein laid a foundation for his salvation: in that it is said the top reached up to heaven, that is to shew that the divine nature was joined to the human, and by that means he was every way made a Saviour complete. Now concerning this ladder, 'tis said, *Heaven* was open where it stood, to show that by him there is entrance into life: 'tis said also concerning this ladder, that the Lord stood there, at the top, above it: saying, 'I am the Lord God of Abraham,' (*Gen.* 28:13), to shew his hearty and willing reception of those that ascend the height of his sanctuary this way. All which Christ further explains by saying, 'I am the way, and the truth, and the life, no man cometh unto the Father, but by me' (*John* 14:6). Look to thyself then, that thou do truly and after the right manner embrace this ladder, so will he *draw* thee up thither after him (*John* 12:32). All the rungs of this ladder are sound and fitly placed, not one of them is set further than that by faith thou mayest ascend step by step unto, even until thou shalt come to the highest step thereof, from whence, or by which thou mayest step in at the celestial gate where thy soul desireth to dwell.

Take my caution then, and be wary, no man can come thither but by him. Thither I say to be accepted: thither, there to dwell, and there to abide with joy for ever.

PART TWO

Desiring the Incomparable

1: *Praying For An Ability*

Having thus spoken of the breadth, the length, and depth, and height, that is in God's mercy by Christ to us-ward; we will now come more directly to the prayer of the Apostle for these Ephesians, with reference thereunto; to wit, that they might be able to comprehend with all saints what they are.

First, as to a prayer for ability, the ability that he prays for, to the end that they may be capable to do this thing.

The weakness that is here supposed to hinder their thus comprehending, &c., did doubtless lie in their grace, as well as their nature: for in both, with reference to them that are Christians, there is great disability, unless they be strengthened mightily by the Holy Ghost. Nature's ability depends upon graces, and the ability of graces, depends upon the mighty help of the Spirit of God. Hence as nature itself, where grace is not, sees nothing; so nature by grace sees but weakly, if that grace is not strengthened with all might by the Spirit of grace. The breadths, lengths, depths and heights here made mention of, are mysteries, and in all their operations, do work wonderfully mysteriously: insomuch that many times, though they are all of them busily engaged for this and the other child of God, yet they themselves see nothing of them. As Christ said to Peter, 'What I do thou knowest not now' (*John* 13:7); so may it be said to many where the grace and mercy of God in Christ is working: they do not know, they understand not what it is, nor what will be the end of such dispensations of God towards them. Wherefore they also say as Peter to Christ, 'Dost thou wash my feet? . . . thou shalt never wash my feet' (*John* 13:6–8). Yea, and when some light to convince of this folly breaks in upon them, yet if it be not very distinct and clear; causing the person to know the true cause, nature, and end of God's doing of this or that, they swerve with Peter, *as much on the other side* (*John* 13:9, 10). They have not known my ways, and my methods with them in this world, were that that caused Israel always to err in their hearts (*Heb.* 3:10) and lie cross to all, and each of these breadths, lengths, depths, and heights, whenever they were under the exercise of any of them in the wilderness.

And the reason is, as I said before, for that they are very mysterious in their workings. For they work by, upon, and against oppositions; for, and in order to the help and salvation of his people. Also (as was hinted a while since) that the power and glory of *this* breadth, and length, &c. of the mercy and grace of God, may the more show its excellency and sufficiency as to our deliverance; we by him seem quite to be delivered up to the breadths, lengths, and depths, and heights that oppose, and that utterly seek our ruin: wherefore at such times, nothing of breadths, lengths, depths, or heights can be seen, save by those that are very well skilled in those mysterious methods of God, in his gracious actings towards his people. 'Who will bring me into the strong city,' and 'wilt not thou, O God, which hadst cast us off? and thou, O God, which didst not go out with our armies?' (*Psa.* 60:9, 10) is a lesson too hard for every Christian man to say over believingly. And what was it that made Jonah say, when he was in the belly of hell, 'Yet I will look again toward thy holy temple' (*Jon.* 2:4), but the good skill that he had in understanding of the mystery of these breadths, and lengths, and depths, and heights of God, and of the way of his working by them. Read the text at large. 'Thou hadst cast me into the deep, in the midst of the seas, and the floods compassed me about. All thy billows and thy waves passed over me. Then I said, I am cast out of thy sight; yet I will look again toward thy holy temple' (*Jon.* 2:3, 4).

These, and such like sentences, are easily played with by a preacher, when in the pulpit, specially if he has a little of the notion of things, but of the *difficulty* and *strait*, that those are brought into, out of whose mouth such things, or words are extorted, by reason of the force of the labyrinths they are fallen into; of *those* they experience nothing, wherefore to those they are utterly strangers.

He then that is able to comprehend with all saints what is the breadth, and length, and depth, and height; must be a good expositor of *providences*, and must see the way, and the workings of God by *them*. Now there are providences of two sorts, seemingly good, and seemingly bad, and those do usually as Jacob did, when he blessed the sons of Joseph, cross hands; and lay the blessing where *we* would not. 'And when Joseph saw that his father laid his right hand upon the head of Ephraim, it displeased him' (*Gen.* 48:17). I say there are providences unto which we would have the blessings entailed, but they are not. And they are providences that smile upon the flesh; to wit, such as cast into the lap, health, wealth, plenty, ease, friends, and abundance of this world's good: because these, [Manasseh, as his name doth signify,] have in them an aptness to make us forget our toil, our low estate, and from whence we were (*Gen.* 41:51) but the great blessing is not in them. There are providences again, that take away from us whatever is desirable to the flesh; such is the sickness, losses, crosses, persecution and affliction; and usually in these, though they make us shudder whenever they come upon us, blessing coucheth, and is ready to help us. For God, as the name of Ephraim signifies, makes us 'fruitful in the land of our affliction' (*Gen.* 41:52). He therefore, in blessing of his people, lays his hands across, guiding them wittingly, and laying the chiefest blessing on the head of Ephraim, or in that providence, that sanctifies affliction. Abel! what, to the reason of Eve was he, in comparison of Cain. Rachel called Benjamin the son of her sorrow: but Jacob knew how to give him a better name (*Gen.* 35:18). Jabez also, though his mother so called him, because, as it seems, she brought him forth with more than ordinary sorrow, was yet more honourable, more godly, than his brethren (*1 Chron.* 4:9, 10). He that has skill to judge of providences aright, has a great ability in him to comprehend with other saints, what is the breadth, and length, and depth, and height: but he that has not skill as to discerning of them, is but a child in his judgment in those *high* and mysterious things. And hence it is, that some shall suck honey out of that, at the which others tremble for fear it should poison them, I have often been made to say, 'Sorrow is better than laughter; and the house of mourning better than the house of mirth' (*Eccles.* 7:3–5). And I have more often seen, that the afflicted are always the best sort of Christians. There is a man, never well, never prospering, never but under afflictions, disappointments and sorrows: why this man, if he be a Christian, is one of the best of men. 'They that go down to the sea, . . . that do business in great waters, these see the works of the Lord, and his wonders in the deep' (*Psa.* 107:23, 24). And it is from hence, for aught I know, that James admonishes the brother of high degree to rejoice in that he is made low. And he renders the reason of it, to wit, for that the fashion of the world perisheth, the rich man fadeth away in his way; but the tempted, and he that endureth temptation is blessed (*James* 1:10–12). Now, I know these things are not excellent in themselves, nor yet to be desired for any profit that they can yield, but God doth use by these, as by a tutor or instructor, to make known to them that are exercised with them, so much of himself as to make them understand *that* riches of his goodness that is seldom by other means broken up to the sons of men. And hence 'tis said, that the afterwards of affliction doth yield the peaceable fruits of righteousness unto them which are exercised thereby (*Heb.* 12:11).

The sum is, *these* breadths, and lengths, and depths, and heights of God, are to be discerned; and some that are good, do more, and some do less discern them, and how they are working, and putting forth themselves in every providence, in every change, in every turn of the wheel that passeth by us in this world. I do not question but that there are some that are alive that have been able to say, the days of affliction have been the best unto them; and that could, if it were lawful, pray that they might always be in affliction, if God would but do to them as he did when his hand was last upon them. For by them he caused his light to shine: Or as Job has it, 'Thou huntest me as a fierce lion: and again thou shewest thyself marvellously upon me' (*Job* 10:16). See also the writing of Hezekiah, and read what profit he found in afflictions (*Isa.* 38).

But again, these breadths, lengths, depths, and heights, have in themselves naturally that glory, that cannot be so well discerned, or kept in view by weak eyes. He had need have an eye like an eagle, that can look upon the sun, that can look upon these great things, and not be stricken blind therewith. You see how Saul was served when he was going to Damascus (*Acts* 9). But Stephen could stand and look up stedfastly into heaven; and that too when with Jonah he was going into the deep (*Acts* 7). But I have done with this, and proceed.

[35]

2: *Praying For An Understanding*

'*That ye may be able to comprehend.*' Although apprehending is included in comprehending; yet to comprehend is more. To comprehend is to know a thing fully; or, to reach it all. But here we must distinguish, and say, that there is a comprehending that is absolute, and a comprehending that is comparative. Of comprehending absolutely, or perfectly, we are not here to speak; for that the Apostle could not, in this place, as to the thing prayed for, desire: For it is utterly impossible perfectly to know whatsoever is in the breadths, lengths, depths, and heights here spoken of. Whether you call them mercies, judgments, or the ways of God with men. 'How unsearchable are his judgments, and his ways past finding out!' (*Rom.* 11:33). Or, if you take them to signify his love, unto which you see I am inclined; why, that you read of in the same place, to be it 'which passes knowledge.' Wherefore should the Apostle by this term, conclude, or insinuate, that what he calls here breadths, lengths, depths, or heights, might be fully, or perfectly understood and known, he would not only contradict other scriptures, but himself, in one and the self same breath. Wherefore it must be understood comparatively; that is, and that he says, with, or as much as others, as any, even with all saints. *That ye may be able to comprehend with all saints, what is the breadth, and length, and depth, and height.* I would ye were as able to understand, to know, and to find out these things, as ever any were; and to know with the very best of saints, *The love of*

Christ, which passeth knowledge. There are, as has before been hinted, degrees of knowledge of these things; some know more, some less; but the Apostle prays that these Ephesians might see, know, and understand as much thereof as the best, or as any under heaven.

(I) A MARK OF THE GOSPEL MINISTER

And this, in the *first* place, shows us the love of a minister of Jesus Christ. A minister's love to his flock is seen in his praying for them: wherefore Paul, commonly, by his epistles, either first or last, or both, gives the churches to understand, That he did often heartily pray to God for them (*Rom.* 16:20, 24; 1 *Cor.* 16:23; *Gal.* 6:18; *Eph.* 1:16; *Phil.* 1:4; *Col.* 1:3; 1 *Thess.* 1:2; 1 *Tim.* 6:21; 2 *Tim.* 4:22). And not only so, but also specifies the mercies, and blessings, and benefits which he earnestly begged for them of God (*2 Cor.* 13:7; 2 *Thess.* 1:11).

(II) AN INDICATION OF BENEFITS AVAILABLE WHICH ARE:

But, *secondly,* This implies that there are great benefits [which] accrue to Christians by the comprehending of these things: Yea, it implies that something very special is ministered to us by this knowledge of these; and here to touch upon a few of them.

a) a sense of God's greatness

He that shall arrive to some competent knowledge of these things, shall understand more thoroughly the greatness, the wisdom, the power, &c. of the God that is above. For by these expressions are the attributes of God set forth unto us: And although I have discoursed of them hitherto under the notion of grace and mercy, yet it was not for that

I concluded, they excluded the expressing of his other attributes, but because they all, as it were, turn into loving methods in the wheel of their heavenly motion towards the children of God. Hence it is said, 'God is love' (*1 John* 4:16). 'God is light' (*1 John* 1:5). God is what he is for his own glory, and the good of them that fear him. God! Why God in the breadth, length, depth, height, that is here intended, comprehends the whole world (*Col.* 1:17). The whole world is *in* him: for he is before, above, beyond, and round about all things. Hence it is said, The heavens for breadth, are but his span: That he gathereth the wind in his fists (*Prov.* 30:4), measureth the waters in the hollow of his hand, weigheth the mountains in scales, and the hills in a balance (*Isa.* 40:12). Yea, that 'all nations before him *are* as nothing, and they are counted to him less than nothing, and vanity' (verse 17). Hence we are said to live and move in him (*Acts* 17:28), and that he is beyond all search.

I will add one word more, notwithstanding there is such a revelation of him in his word, in the book of creatures, and in the book of providences; yet the Scripture says, 'Lo, these *are* parts of his ways: but how little a portion is heard of him?' (*Job* 26:14). So great is God above all that we have read, heard, or seen of him, either in the Bible, in heaven, or earth, the sea, or what else is to be understood. But now, That a poor mortal, a lump of sinful flesh, or, as the scripture-phrase is, poor *dust and ashes*, should be in the favour, in the heart, and wrapped up in the compassions of SUCH a God! Oh amazing! O astonishing consideration! And yet 'This God is our God for ever and ever; and He will be our guide even unto death' (*Psa.* 48:14).

It is said of our God, 'That he humbleth himself when he beholds things in heaven.' How much more then when he openeth his eyes upon man; but most of all when he makes it, as one may say, his business to visit him every morning, and to try him every moment, having set his heart upon him, being determined to set him also among his princes. 'The Lord is high above all nations, and his glory above the heavens. Who is like unto the Lord our God, who dwelleth on high, Who humbleth himself to behold the things that are in heaven, and in the earth! He raiseth up the poor out of the dust, and lifteth the needy out of the dunghill; that he may set him with princes, even with the princes of his people' (*Psa.* 113:3–8).

b) a confidence before the world

If *this* God be our God; or if our God be such a God, and could we but attain to *that* knowledge of the breadth, and length, and depth, and height that is in him, as the Apostle here prays, and desires we may, we should never be afraid of anything we shall meet with, or that shall assault us in this world. The great God, the former of all things, taketh part with them that fear him, and that engage themselves to walk in his ways, of love, and respect, they bear unto him; so that such may boldly say, 'The Lord *is* my helper, and I will not fear what man shall do unto me' (*Heb.* 13:6). Would it not be amazing, should you see a man encompassed with chariots and horses, and weapons for his defence, yet afraid of being sparrow blasted, or over-run by a grasshopper! Why, '*It is* he that sitteth upon the circle of the earth, and' to whom 'the inhabitants thereof are as grasshoppers' (*Isa.* 40:22), that is the God of the people that are lovers of Jesus Christ; therefore we should not fear them. To fear man, is to forget God; and to be careless in a time of danger, is to forget God's ordinance. What is it then? Why, let us fear God, and diligently keep his way, with what prudence and regard to our preservation, and also the preservation of what we have, we may: And if, we doing this, our God shall deliver us, and what we have, into the hands of them that hate us, let us laugh, be fearless and careless, not minding *now* to do anything else but to stand up for him against the workers of iniquity; fully concluding, that both we, and our enemies, are in the hand of him that loveth his people, and that will certainly render a reward to the wicked, after that he has sufficiently tried us by their means. 'The great God that formed all things, both rewardeth the fool, and rewardeth transgressors' (*Prov.* 26:10).

c) a reverence before God
Another thing that the knowledge of what is prayed for of the Apostle, if we attain it, will minister to us, is, *An holy fear and reverence of this great God in our souls*; both because he is great, and because he is wise and good (*Jer.* 10:7). 'Who shall not fear thee, O Lord, and glorify thy name?' (*Rev.* 15:4).

Greatness should beget fear, greatness should beget reverence: Now who so great as our God; and so, who to be feared like him! He also is wise, and will not be deceived by any. 'He will bring evil, and not call back his words, but will rise against the house of evil-doers, and against the help of them that work iniquity (*Isa.* 31:2). Most men deal with God as if he were not wise; as if he either knew not the wickedness of their hearts and ways, or else knew not how to be even with them for it: When, alas! he is *wise* in heart, and *mighty* in power; and although he will not, without cause, afflict, yet he will not let wickedness go unpunished. This therefore should make us fear. He also is *good*, and this should make us serve him with fear. Oh! that a great God should be a good God; a good God to an unworthy, to an undeserving, and to a people that continually do what they can to provoke the eyes of his glory; this should make us tremble. He is fearful in service, fearful in praises.

The *breadth*, and *length*, and *depth*, and *height* of his out-going towards the children of men, should also beget in us a very great fear and dread of his majesty. When the prophet saw the height of the wheels, he said they were *dreadful* (*Ezek.* 1:18), and cried out unto them, *O wheel!* (10:13). His judgments also are a great deep (*Psa.* 36:6); nor is there any 'searching of his understanding' (*Isa.* 40:28). He can tell how to bring his *wheel* upon us; and to make our table a snare, a trap, and a stumbling-block unto us (*Isa.* 8:14; *Rom.* 11:8–10). He can tell how to make his Son to us a rock of offence, and his gospel to be a savour of death unto death, unto us (*2 Cor.* 2:15, 16). He can tell how to choose delusions for us (*Isa.* 66:4; *2 Thess.* 2:11, 12) and to lead us forth with the workers of iniquity (*Psa.* 125:5). He can out-wit, and out-do us, and prevail against us for ever (*Job* 14:20); and therefore we should be afraid and fear before him, for our good, and the good of ours for ever: Yea, it is for these purposes, with others, that the Apostle prayeth thus for this people: For the comprehending of these things, do poise and keep the heart in an even course. This yields comfort; this gives encouragment; this begets fear and reverence in our hearts of God.

d) a willingness that he should be our God
Yea, he will also make us abide by that willingness. Jacob said with a vow, 'If God will be with me, and will keep me in this way that I go, and will give me bread to eat, and raiment to put on, so that I come again to my father's house in peace; then shall the LORD be my God: And this stone, which I have set *for* a pillar, shall be God's house: and of all that thou shalt give me I will surely give the tenth unto thee' (*Gen.* 28:20–22). Thus he considered the great-ness of God, and from a supposition that he was what he had heard him, of his father, to be; he concluded to choose him for his God, and that he would worship him, and give

him that honour that was due to him as God. How did the king of Babylon set him above all gods, when but some sparkling rays from him did light upon him: he calls him 'a God of gods' (*Dan.* 2:47), prefers him above all gods, charges all people and nations that they do nothing amiss against him (*Dan.* 3:28, 29): he calls him 'the most high' God, the God 'that liveth for ever'; and confesses, that he doth whatsoever he will in heaven and earth; and concludes with praising and extolling of him (*Dan.* 4). We naturally love greatness; and when the glorious beauty of the King of glory shall be manifest to us, and we shall behold it, we shall say as Joshua did; Let all men do as seems them good; but I, and my house will serve the Lord (*Josh.* 24:15).

When the Apostle Paul sought to win the Athenians to him, he sets him forth before them with such terms as bespeaks his greatness; calling of him (and that rightly) 'God that made the world, and all things: . . . the Lord of heaven and earth; . . . One that giveth to all life and breath, and all things;' One that is nigh to every one; 'he in whom we live, and move, and have our being:' God that hath made of one blood all nations of men, and that hath determined the times before appointed, and the bounds of their habitation, (*Acts* 17:24–28). These things bespeak the greatness of God, and are taking to considering men. Yea, these very Athenians, while ignorant of him, from those dark hints that they had by natural light concerning him, erected an altar to him, and put this singular inscription upon it, 'To the unknown God:' to show, that according to their mode, they had some kind of reverence for him: but how much more when they came to know him? and to believe that God, in all his greatness, had engaged himself to be theirs; and to bring them to himself, that they might in time be partakers of his glory.

e) a better grasp of the glory to come

The more a man knows, or understands of the greatness of
God towards him, expressed here by the terms of unsearchable breadth, length, depth, and height; the better
will he be able in his heart to conceive of the excellent
glory and greatness of the things that are laid up in the
heavens for them that fear him. They that know nothing
of this greatness, know nothing of them; they that think
amiss of this greatness, think amiss of them; they that
know but little of this greatness, know but little of them:
But he that is able to comprehend with all saints what is
the *breadth*, and *length*, and *depth*, and *height*; he is best
able to conceive of, and, consequently to make a judgment
concerning the due worth, and blessed glory of them.

This is both evident to reason; also experience con-
firmeth the same. For, as for those *dark souls* that know
nothing of his greatness, they have in derision those who
are, through the splendour of the glory, captivated and
carried away after God. Also, those whose judgments are
corrupted, and themselves thereby made as drunkards, to
judge of things foolishly, they, as it were, step in the same
steps with the other, and vainly imagine thereabout.
Moreover, we shall see those little-spirited Christians,
though Christians indeed, that are but in a small measure
acquainted with this God, with the breadths, and lengths,
and depths, and heights that are in him, taken but little
with the glory and blessedness that they are to go to when
they die: wherefore they are neither so mortified to this
world, so dead to sin, so self-denying, so delighted in the
book of God, nor so earnest in desires to be acquainted
with the heights, and depths that are therein. No, this is
reserved only for those who are devoted thereto; who have
been acquainted with God in a measure beyond that which
your narrow-spirited Christians understand. There doth
want as to these things, enlargings in the hearts of the most

of saints, as there did in those of Corinth, and also in those at Ephesus: Wherefore, as Paul bids the one, and prays that the other may be enlarged, and have great knowledge thereabout: so we should, to answer such love, through desire, separate ourselves from earthly things that we may seek and intermeddle with all wisdom (*Prov.* 18:1). Christ says, 'If any man will do his will, he shall know of the doctrine' (*John* 7:17; *Isa.* 28:9). Oh! that we were *indeed* enlarged as to these breadths, and lengths, and depths, and heights of God, as the Apostle desired the Ephesians might.

f) a sure conviction of the end of all things

Knowing God, those great truths; the coming of Christ, the resurrection of the dead, and eternal judgment, would neither seem so like fables, nor be so much off our hearts as they do, and are (*1 Cor.* 15:35). For the thorough belief of them depends upon the knowledge of the abilities that are in God to perform what he has said thereabout: And hence it is that your inferior sort of Christians live so like, as if none of these things were at hand; and hence it is again, that they so soon are shaken in mind about them, when tempted of the devil, or briskly assaulted by deceivers. But this cometh to pass that there may be fulfilled what is written: 'And while the bridegroom tarried, they all slumbered and slept' (*Matt.* 25:1–7). Surely, the meaning is, they were asleep about his coming, the resurrection and the judgment; and, consequently had lost much of that knowledge of God, the which if they had retained; these truths, with power, would have been upon their hearts. The Corinthians were horribly decayed here, though some more than others: Hence Paul, when he treats of this doctrine, bids them 'awake to righteousness,' and not sin, telling them, that some among them had not the knowledge of God (*1 Cor.* 15:34). To be sure, they had not such a knowledge of God as would keep them steady in the faith of these things (verse 51).

Now, the knowledge of the things above-mentioned, to wit, 'this comprehending knowledge;' will enlarge these things, bring them near, and make them to be credited as are the greatest of God's truths: and the virtue of the faith of them is, to make one die daily.

g) a greater longing for heaven

Another advantage that floweth from this knowledge, is, that it makes the next world desirable, not simply as it is with those *lean souls*, that desire it only as the thief desireth the judge's favour, that he may be saved from the halter; but out of love such have to God and to the beauties of the house he dwells in; and that they may be rid of this world, which is to such as a dark dungeon. The knowledge of God that men pretend they have, may easily be judged of, by the answerable or unanswerableness of their hearts and lives thereto. Where is the man that groans earnestly to be gone to God, that counts this life a strait unto him: that saith as a sick man of my acquaintance did, when his friend at his bed-side prayed to God to spare his life, *No, no,* said he, *pray not so; for it is better to be dissolved and be gone.* Christians should show the world how they believe; not by words on paper, not by gay and flourishing notions (*James* 2:18): but by those desires they have to be gone, and the proof that these desires are true, is a life in heaven while we are on earth (*Phil.* 3:20, 21). I know words are cheap, but a dram of grace is worth all the world. But where, as I said, shall it be found, not among carnal men, not among weak Christians, but among those, and those only, that enjoy a great measure of Paul's wish here.

3: *Praying For A Knowledge*

'*And to know the love of Christ which passeth knowledge,*' –
These words are the second part of the text, and they deal
mainly about the love of Christ, who is the Son of God. We
have spoken already briefly of God, and therefore now we
shall speak also of his Son. These words are a part of the
prayer afore-mentioned, and have something of the same
strain in them. In the first part, he prays that they might
comprehend that which cannot absolutely by any means
be comprehended: and here he prays that that might be
known, which yet in the same breath he saith, *passeth
knowledge*, to wit, the love of Christ. *And to know the love
of Christ, which passeth knowledge.* In the words we are to
take notice of three things:

FIRST, Of the love of Christ.
SECOND, Of the exceeding greatness of it.
THIRD, Of the knowledge of it.

(I) OF THE LOVE OF CHRIST

We will begin with the first of these, to wit, *Of the love of
Christ*. Now for the explication of this we must inquire
into three things, *First*, Who Christ is. *Second*, What love
is. *Third*, What the love of Christ is.

a) *Who Christ is*
First, Christ is a person of no less quality than he is of
whom we treated before: to wit, *very God*. So I say, not

titularly, not *nominally*, not so *counterfeitly*, but the self-same in *nature* with the Father (*John* 1:1, 2; *1 John* 5.7; *Phil.* 2:6). Wherefore what we have under consideration, is so much the more to be taken notice of; namely, that a person so great, so high, so glorious, as this Jesus Christ was, should have love for us, that passes knowledge. It is common for equals to love, and for superiors to be beloved; but for the King of princes, for the Son of God, for Jesus Christ to love *man* thus: this is amazing, and that so much the more, for that man the object of this love, is so low, so mean, so vile, so undeserving, and so inconsiderable, as by the Scriptures, everywhere he is described to be.

But to speak a little more particularly of this person. He is called God (*John* 1:1). The King of glory (*Psa.* 24:10) and Lord of glory (*1 Cor.* 2:8). The brightness of the glory of his Father (*Heb.* 1:3). The head over all things (*Eph.* 1:22). The Prince of life (*Acts* 3:15). The Creator of all things (*Col.* 1:16). The upholder of all things (*Heb.* 1:3). The disposer of all things (*Matt.* 28:18). The only beloved of the Father (*Matt.* 11).

But the persons of him beloved, are called transgressors, sinners, enemies, dust and ashes, fleas (*1 Sam.* 24:14), worms, shadows, vapours: vile, sinful, filthy, unclean, ungodly fools, madmen. And now is it not to be wondered at, and are we not to be affected herewith, saying, And wilt thou set thine eye upon such a one? But how much more when *he* will set his *heart* upon us. And yet this great, this high, this glorious person, verily, verily loveth such.

b) What love is
Second, We now come to the second thing, namely, *to shew what is love*; not in a way of nice distinction of words, but in a plain and familiar discourse, yet respecting the love of the person under consideration.

[47]

Love ought to be considered with reference to the subject as well as to the object of it.

The subject of love in the text, is Christ; but forasmuch as love *in him* is diverse from the love that is *in us*; therefore it will not be amiss, if a little [of] the difference be made appear.

Love in us is a passion of the soul, and being such, is subject to *ebb* and *flow*, and to be extreme both ways. For whatever is a passion of the soul, whether love or hatred, joy or fear, is more apt to exceed, or come short, than to keep within its due bounds. Hence, oft-times that which is loved today is hated to-morrow (*2 Sam.* 13:15); yea, and that which should be loved with bounds of moderation, is loved to the drowning of both soul and body in perdition and destruction (*1 Tim.* 6:9, 10).

Besides, love in us is apt to choose to itself undue and unlawful objects, and to reject those, that with leave of God, we may embrace and enjoy; so unruly, as to the laws and rules of divine government, oft-times is this passion of love in us.

Love in us, requires, that something pleasing and delightful be in the object loved, at least, so it must appear to the lust and fancy of the person loving, or else love cannot act; for the love that is in us, is not of power to set itself on work, where no allurement is in the thing to be beloved.

Love in us decays, though once never so warm and strongly fixed, if the object falls off, as to its first alluring provocation; or disappointeth our expectation with some unexpected reluctancy to our fancy or our mind.

All this we know to be true from nature, for every one of us are thus; nor can we refuse, or choose as to love, but upon, and after the rate, and the working thus of our passions. Wherefore our love, as we are natural, is weak, unorderly, fails and miscarries, either by being too much or too little; yea, though the thing which is beloved be allowed for an object of love, both by the law of nature and grace. We therefore must put a vast different betwixt love, as found in us, and love as found in Christ, and that, both as to the nature, principle, or object of love.

Love in Christ is not love of the same nature, as is love in us; love in him is essential to his being (*1 John* 4:16) but in us it is not so, as has been already showed. God is love; Christ is God; therefore Christ is love, *love naturally*. Love therefore is essential to his being. He may as well cease to *be*, as cease to *love*. Hence therefore it follows, that love in Christ floweth not from so low and beggarly a principle, as doth love in man; and consequently is not, nor can be attended with those infirmities or defects, that the love of man is attended with.

It is not attended with those unruly or uncertain motions that ours is attended with: here is no ebbing, no flowing, no going beyond, no coming short; and so nothing of uncertainty. 'Having loved his own which were in the world, he loved them unto the end' (*John* 13:1).

True, there is a way of manifesting of this love, which is suited to our capacities, as men, and by that we see it sometimes more, sometimes less (*Song of Sol.* 7:11, 12): also it is manifested to us as we *do*, or do *not* walk with God in this world (*John* 14:23). I speak now of saints.

Love in Christ pitcheth not itself upon undue or unlawful objects; nor refuseth to embrace what by the eternal covenant is made capable thereof. It always acteth according to God; nor is there at any time the least shadow of swerving as to this.

Love in Christ requireth no taking beauteousness in the object to be beloved, as not being able to put forth itself without such attracting allurements (*Ezek.* 16:6–8). It can act *of* and *from* itself, without all such dependencies. This is manifest to all who have the least true knowledge of what that object is in itself, on which the Lord Jesus has set his heart to love him.

Love in Christ decays not, nor can be tempted so to do by anything that happens, or that shall happen hereafter, in the object so beloved. But as this love at first acts by, and from itself, so it continueth to do until all things that are imperfections, are completely and everlastingly subdued. The reason is, because Christ loves to make us comely, *not* because we *are* so (*Ezek.* 16:9–14).

Objection. But all along Christ compareth his love to ours; now, why doth he so, if they be so much unlike?

Answer. Because we know not love but by the passions of love that work in our hearts; wherefore he condescends to our capacities, and speaketh of his love to us, according as we find love to work in ourselves to others. Hence he sets forth his love to us, by borrowing from us instances of our love to wife and children (*Eph.* 5.25). Yea, he sometimes sets forth his love to us, by calling to our mind how sometimes a man loves a woman that is a whore, 'Go,' (saith God to the prophet) 'love a woman beloved of her friend, yet an adulteress, according to the word of the Lord toward the children of Israel, who look to other gods, and love flagons of wine' (*Hos.* 3:1). But then, these things must not be understood with respect to the nature, but the dispensations and manifestations of love; no, nor with reference to these neither, any further than by making use of such suitable similitudes, thereby to commend his love to us, and thereby to beget in us affections to him for the love bestowed upon us.

Wherefore Christ's love must be considered both with respect to the essence, and also as to the divers workings of it. For the essence thereof, it is as I said, natural with himself, and as such, it is the root and ground of all those actions of his, whereby he hath showed that himself is loving to sinful man. But now, though the love that is in him is essential to his nature, and can vary no more than God himself: yet we see not this love but by the fruits of it, nor can it otherwise be discerned. 'Hereby perceive we the love of God, because he laid down his life for us' (*1 John* 3:16). We must then betake ourselves to the discoveries of this love, of which there are two sorts; [namely,] such as are the foundations, and such as are the consequences of those fundamental acts. Those which I call the foundations, are they upon which all other discoveries of his goodness depend, and they are two. 1. His dying for us. 2. His improving of his death for us at the right hand of God.

c) What the love of Christ is which is made known:
And this leads me to the third particular, to wit, to shew you *what the love of Christ is*; namely, in the discovery of it. *And to know the love of Christ.*

The love of Christ is made known unto us, as I said,

(i) By his actual dying for us. This appears to be *wonderful in itself*, and that both with respect to the nature of that death, as also, with respect to the persons for whom he so died.

The love of Christ appears to be wonderful by the death he died: In that *he died*, in that he died *such* a death. 'Twas strange love in Christ that moved him to die for us: strange, because not according to the custom of the world. Men do not use, in cool blood, deliberately to come upon the stage or ladder, to lay down their lives for others; but this did Jesus Christ, and that too for such, whose qualification, if it be duly considered, will make this act of his, far more amazing, *He laid down his life for his enemies* (*Rom.* 5), and for those that could not abide him; yea, for those, even for those that brought him to the cross: not accidentally, or because it happened so, but knowingly, designedly (*Zech.* 12:10), he knew it was for those he

[51]

died, and yet his love led him to lay down his life for them. I will add, That those very people for whom he laid down his life, though they by all sorts of carriages did what they could to provoke him to pray to God his Father, that he would send and cut them off by the flaming sword of angels (*Matt.* 26:53) he would not be provoked, but would lay down his life for them. Nor must I leave off here: We never read that Jesus Christ was more cheerful in all his life on earth, than when he was going to lay down his life for them, now he thanked God (*Luke* 22:19), now he sang (*Matt.* 26:30).

But this is not all. He did not only die, but died *such a death*, as indeed cannot be expressed. He was content to be counted the *sinner*: yea, to be counted the *sin* of the sinner, nor could this but be odious to so holy a Lamb as he was, yet willing to be *this* and *thus* for that love that he bare to men.

This being thus, it follows, that his sufferings must be unconceivable; for that, what in justice was the proper wages of sin and sinners, he must undergo; and what that was can no man so well know as he himself and damned spirits; for the proper wages of sin, and of sinners for their sin, is that death which layeth pains, *such* pains which it deserveth upon the man that dieth so: But Christ died so, and consequently was seized by those pains not only in body but in soul. His tears, his cries, his bloody sweat (*Luke* 22:44), the hiding of his Father's face; yea, God's forsaking of him in his extremity (*Matt.* 27:46), plainly enough declares the nature of the death he died (*Mark* 25:39). For my part, I stand amazed at those that would not have the world believe, that the death of Jesus Christ was, in itself, so terrible as it was.

I will not stand here to discourse the place called *Hell*, where the spirits of the damned are, we are discoursing of the nature of Christ's sufferings: and I say, if Christ was put into the very capacity of one that must suffer what in justice ought to be inflicted for sin; then, how we can so diminish the greatness of his sufferings, as some do, without undervaluing of the greatness of his love, I know not; and how they will answer it, I know not.

And on the contrary, what if I should say, that the soul of Christ suffered as long as his body lay in the grave, and that God's loosing of the pains of death at Christ's resurrection, must not so much be made mention of with reference to his body, as to his soul, if to his body at all. For what pain of death was his body capable of, when his soul was separate from it? (*Acts* 2:24). And yet God's loosing the pains of death, seems to be but an immediate antecedent to his rising from the dead. And this sense Peter doth indeed seem to pursue, saying, 'For David speaketh concerning him; I foresaw the Lord always before my face, for he is on my right hand, that I should not be moved. Therefore did my heart rejoice, and my tongue was glad; moreover also my flesh shall rest in hope, because thou wilt not leave my soul in hell, neither wilt thou suffer thine holy one to see corruption' (*Acts* 2:25–27). This, saith Peter, was not spoken of David, but he, being a prophet, and knowing that God had sworn with an oath, that of the fruit of his loins according to the flesh he would raise up Christ to sit on his throne. He seeing this before, spake of the resurrection of Christ, that his soul was not left in hell, neither did his flesh see corruption (verses 29–31). 'Thou wilt not leave my soul in hell;' his soul was not left in hell. Of what use are these expressions, if the soul of Christ suffered not, if it suffered not when separated from the body? for of that time the Apostle Peter seems to treat. Besides, if it be not improper to say, that soul was not left there, that never was there, I am at a loss. *Thou wilt not* leave, his soul was *not left there; ergo*, It was there, seems to be the natural conclusion. If it be objected, that by *hell* is meant the grave, 'tis foolish to think that the soul of Christ lay there while his body lay dead therein. But again, the Apostle seems clearly to distinguish between the places where the soul and body of Christ were; counting his body to be in the grave, and his soul, for the time, in hell. If there be objected what was said by him to the thief upon the cross (*Luke* 23:43), I can answer, Christ might speak that with reference to his God-head, and if so, that lies as no objection to what hath been insinuated. And why may not that be so understood, as well as where he said, when on earth, 'The Son of man which is in heaven' (*John* 3:13), meaning himself. For the personality of the Son of God, call him Son of man, or what other term is fitting, resideth not in the human, but divine nature of Jesus Christ. However, since hell is sometimes taken for the place (*Acts* 1:25), sometimes for the grave, sometimes for the state (*Psa.* 116:3), and sometimes but for a figure of the place where the damned are tormented (*Jon.* 2:2); I will not strictly assign to Christ the place, the prison where the damned spirits are (*1 Pet.* 3:19), but will say, as I said before, that he was put into the place of sinners, into the sins of sinners, and received what by justice was the proper wages of sin both in body and soul: As is evident from that fifty-third of Isaiah (verses 10, 11). This soul of his I take to be that which the *inwards* and the *fat* of the burnt sacrifices was a figure, or shadow of. 'And the fat and the inwards were burnt upon the altar, whilst the body was burned for sin without the camp' (*Exod.* 29:13, 14; *Lev.* 8:14–17).

And now having said this much, wherein have I derogated from the glory and holiness of Christ? Yea, I have endeavoured to set forth something of the greatness of his sorrows, the odiousness of sin, the nature of justice, and the love of Christ. And be sure, by how much the sufferings of the Son of God abounded for us, by so much was this unsearchable love of Christ made manifest. Nor can they that would, before the people, pare away, and make but little these infinite sufferings of our Lord, make his love to be so great as they ought, let them use what rhetoric they can. For their objecting the odious names and place of hell, accounting it not to be fit to say, That so holy a person as the Son of God was there. I answer, though I have not asserted it, yet let me ask, which is more odious, hell or sin? Or whether such think that Christ Jesus was subject to be tainted by the badness of the place, had he been there? Or whether, when the scripture says, God is in hell, it is any disparagement to him? (*Psa.* 139:8). Or if a man should be so bold as to say so, Whether by so saying, he confineth Christ to that place for ever? And whether by so thinking he has contradicted that called the *Apostles' creed?*

(ii) By his preparations for dying. Having thus spoken of the death and sufferings of Christ, I shall in the next place speak of *his preparations for his so suffering* for us; and by so doing, yet shew you something more of the greatness of his love.

Christ, as I have told you, was even before his sufferings, a person of no mean generation, being the Son of the eternal God: Neither had his Father any more *such* sons but he; consequently he of right was heir of all things, and so to have dominion over all worlds. For, 'for him were all things created' (*Col.* 1:16). And hence all creatures are subject to him; yea the angels of God worship him (*Heb.* 1). Wherefore as *so* considered, he augmented not his state by becoming lower than the angels for us, for what can be added to him, that is naturally God. Indeed he did take, for our sakes, the human nature into union with himself, and so began to manifest his glory; and the kindness that he had for us before all worlds, began now eminently to show itself. Had this Christ of God, our friend, given all he had to save us, had not his love been wonderful? But when he shall give for us *himself*, this is more wonderful. But this is not all, the case was so betwixt God and man, that this Son of God could not, as he was before the world was, give himself a ransom for us, he being altogether incapable so to do, being such an one as could not be subject to death, the condition that we by sin had put ourselves into.

Wherefore that which would have been a death to some, to wit, the laying aside of glory and becoming, of the King of princes, a servant of the meanest form; this he of his own good-will, was heartily content to do. Wherefore, he that once was the object of the fear of angels, is now become a *little* creature, a worm, an inferior one (*Psa.* 22:6), born of a woman, brought forth in a stable, laid in a manger (*Luke* 2:7), scorned of men, tempted of devils (*Luke* 4:2), was beholden to his creatures for food, for raiment, for harbour, and a place wherein to lay his head when dead. In a word, he 'made himself of no reputation, took upon him the form of a servant, and was made in the likeness of men' (*Phil.* 2:7), that he might become capable to do this kindness for us. And it is worth your noting, that all the while that he was in the world, putting himself upon those other preparations which were to be antecedent to his being made a sacrifice for us, no man, though he told what he came about to many, had, as we read of, an heart once to thank him for what he came about (*Isa.* 53:3). No, they railed on him, they degraded him, they called him devil, they said he was mad, and a deceiver, a blasphemer of God, and a rebel against the state: They accused him to the governor; yea, one of his disciples sold him, another denied him, and they all forsook him, and left him to shift for himself in the hands of his horrible enemies; who beat him with their fists, spat on him, mocked him, crowned him with thorns, scourged him, made a gazing stock of him, and finally, hanged him up by the hands and the feet alive, and gave him vinegar to increase his affliction, when he complained that his anguish had made him thirsty. And yet all this could not take his heart off the work of our redemption. To die he *came*, die he *would*, and die he *did* before he made his return to the Father, for our sins, that we might live through him.

Nor may what we read of in the word concerning those *temporal* sufferings that he underwent be over-looked, and passed by without serious consideration; they being a part of the curse that our sin had deserved! For all temporal plagues are due to our sin while we live, as well as the curse of God to everlasting perdition, when we die. Wherefore this is the reason why the whole life of the Lord Jesus was such a life of affliction and sorrow, he therein bare our sicknesses, and took upon him our deserts: So that now the curse in temporals, as well as the curse in spirituals, and of everlasting malediction, is removed by him away from God's people; and since he overcame them, and got to the cross, it was by reason of the worthiness of the humble obedience that he yielded to his Father's law in our flesh. For his whole life (as well as his death) was a life of merit and purchase, and desert. Hence it is said, 'he increased in favour with God' (*Luke* 2:52). For his works made him still more acceptable to him: For he standing in the room of man, and becoming our reconciler to God; by the heavenly majesty he was counted as such, and so got for us what he earned by his mediatory works; and also partook thereof as he was our head himself. And was there not in all these things love, and love that was infinite? Love which was not essential to his divine nature, could never have carried him through so great a work as this: Passions here would have failed, would have retreated, and have given the recoil; yea, his very humanity would here have flagged and fainted, had it not been managed, governed, and strengthened by his eternal Spirit. Wherefore it is said, that 'through the eternal Spirit he offered himself without spot to God' (*Heb.* 9:14). And that he was declared to be the Son of God, with so doing, and by the resurrection from the dead (*Rom.* 1:4).

(iii) By his achievements through dying we come now to the third thing propounded, and by which his love is discovered, and that is *his improving of his dying for us*. But I must crave pardon of my reader, if he thinks that I can discover the ten hundred thousandth part thereof, for it is impossible; but my meaning is, to give a few hints what beginnings of improvement he made thereof, in order to his further progress therein.

a) He has reconciled every one of the elect Therefore, This his death for us, was so virtuous, that in the space of three days and three nights, it reconciled to God in the body of his flesh as a common person, all, and every one of God's elect. Christ, when he addressed himself to die, presented himself to the justice of the law, as a *common* person; standing in the stead, place, and room of all that he undertook for; He gave 'his life a ransom for many' (*Matt.* 20:28). 'He came into the world to save sinners' (*1 Tim.* 1:15). And as he thus presented himself, so God, his Father, admitted him to this work; and therefore it is said, 'The Lord laid upon him the iniquity of us all:' And again, 'Surely he hath borne our griefs, and carried our sorrows' (*Isa.* 53:4, 6, 12). Hence it unavoidably follows, that whatever he felt, and underwent in the manner, or nature, or horribleness of the death he died, he felt and underwent all as a common person; that is, as he stood in the stead of others: Therefore it is said, 'He was wounded for our transgressions, and bruised for our iniquities;' and that 'the chastisement of our peace was upon him' (*Isa.* 53:5). And again 'the just died for the unjust' (*1 Pet.* 3:18).

Now then, if he presented himself as a common person to justice, if God so admitted and accounted him, if also he laid the sins of the people, whose persons he represented, upon him, and under that consideration punishes him with those punishments and death, that he died. Then Christ in life and death is concluded by the Father to live and die as a common or public person, representing all in this life and death, for whom he undertook *thus* to live, and *thus* to die. So then, it must needs be, that what next befalls this common person, it befalls him with respect to them in whose room and place he stood and suffered. Now, the next that follows, is, 'that he is justified of God:' That is, acquitted and discharged from this punishment, for the sake of the worthiness of his death and merits; for that must be before he could be raised from the dead (*Acts* 2:24). God raised him not up as guilty, to justify him afterwards: His resurrection was the declaration of his precedent justification. He was raised from the dead, because it was neither in equity or justice possible that he should be holden longer there, his merits procured the contrary.

Now he was condemned of God's law, and died by the hand of justice, he was acquitted by God's law, and justified of justice; and all as a common person; so then, in his acquitting, we are acquitted, in his justification we are justified; and therefore the apostle applieth God's justifying of Christ to himself; and that rightly (*Isa.* 50:8;-*Rom.* 3:23, 24). For if Christ be my undertaker, will stand in my place, and do for me, 'tis but reasonable that I should be a partaker: Wherefore we are also said to be 'quickened together with him' (*Eph.* 2:5). That is, when he was quickened in the grave; raised up together, and made to sit together in heavenly places *in* Christ Jesus. Therefore another scripture saith, 'Hath he quickened you . . . together with him, having forgiven you all trespasses' (*Col.* 2:13). *This quickening*, must not be understood of the renovation of our hearts, but of the restoring of Jesus Christ to life after he was crucified; and we are said to be quickened together with him, because we were quickened in him at his death, and were to fall or stand by him quite through the three days and three nights work; and were to take therefore our lot with him: Wherefore it is said again, That his resurrection is our justification (*Rom.* 4:25). That by one offering he has purged our sins for ever (*Heb.* 10:12); and that by his death he hath 'delivered us from the wrath to come' (*1 Thess.* 1:10). But I say, I would be understood aright: This life resideth yet in the Son, and is communicated from him to us, as we are called to believe his word; mean while we are secured from wrath and hell, being justified in his justification, quickened in his quickening, raised up in his resurrection; and made to sit already together in heavenly places in Christ Jesus!

And is not this a glorious improvement of his death, that after two days the whole body of the elect, in him, should be revived, and that in the third day we should live in the sight of God, in and by him (*Heb.* 6:18–20).

b) He has destroyed all their infernal foes. Another improvement of his death for us, was this, By that he slew for us, our infernal foes; by it he abolished death (*2 Tim.* 1:1); by death he destroyed him that had the power of death (*Heb.* 2:14). By death he took away the sting of death (*1 Cor.* 15:55, 56); by death he made death a pleasant sleep to saints, and the grave for a while, an easy house and home for the body. By death he made death such an advantage to us, that it is become a means of translating of the souls of them that believe in him, to life. And all this is manifest, for that death is ours, a blessing to us, as well as Paul and Apollos, the world and life itself (*1 Cor.* 3:22). And that all this is done for us by his death, is apparent, for that his person is where it is, and that by himself as a common person he had got the victory for us. For though as yet all things are not put under our feet, yet we see Jesus crowned with honour and glory, who by the grace of God tasteth death for every man. 'For it became God, for whom *are* all things, and by whom *are* all things, to make the captain of their salvation perfect through sufferings' (*Heb.* 2:7–10). *It became him*; that is, it was but just and right, he should do so; if there was enough in the virtuousness of his death and blood to require such a thing. But there was so. Wherefore God has exalted him, and us in him, above these infernal foes. Let us therefore see ourselves delivered from death first, by the exaltation of our Jesus, let us behold him I say as crowned with glory and honour, as, or because, he tasted death for us. And then we shall see ourselves already in heaven by our head, our undertaker, our Jesus, our Saviour.

c) He has obtained the Holy Spirit for his people Another improvement that has already been made of his death for us, is thus, he hath at his entrance into the presence of God, for his worthiness sake, obtained that the Holy Ghost should be given unto him for us, that we by that might in all things, yet to be done, be made meet to be partakers *personally*, in ourselves, as well as *virtually* by our head and forerunner, of the inheritance of the saints in light. Wherefore the abundant pourings out of what was withheld until the resurrection, and glorification of our Lord Jesus. 'For the Holy Ghost was not yet given, because that Jesus was not yet glorified' (*John* 7:39). Nor was it given so soon as received: for he received it upon his entering into the holy place, when he had sprinkled the mercy seat with the blood of sprinkling, but it was not given out to us till sometime after (*Acts* 4): however it was obtained before (*Acts* 2:32, 33). And it was meet that it should in that infinite immeasurableness in which he received it, first abide upon him, that his human nature, which was the first fruits of the election of God, might receive by its abidings upon him, that glory for which it was ordained; and that we might receive, as we receive all other things, first by our head and undertaker, sanctification in the fulness of it. Hence it is written, that as he is made unto us of God, wisdom, and righteousness, and redemption, so *sanctification* too (*1 Cor.* 1:30). For first we are sanctified *in* his flesh, as we are justified by his righteousness. Wherefore he is that holy one that setteth us, in himself, a holy lump before God, not only with reference to justification and life, but with reference to sanctification and holiness: For we that are elect, are all considered in him as he has received that, as well as in that he has taken possession of the heaven for us. I count not this all the benefit that accrueth to us by Jesus' receiving the Holy Ghost, at his entrance into the presence of God for us: For we also are to receive it ourselves from him, according as by God we are placed in the body at the times appointed of the Father. That we, as was said, may receive personal quickening, personal renovation, personal sanctification; and in conclusion, glory. But I say, for that he hath received this holy Spirit to himself, he received it as the effect of his ascension, which was the effect of his resurrection, and of the merit of his death and passion. And he received it as a common person, as a head and undertaker for the people.

d) He has become Lord of all for them. Another improvement that has been made of his death, and of the merits thereof for us, is that he has obtained to be made of God, the chief and high Lord of heaven and earth, for us, (All this while we speak of the exaltation of the human nature, in, by, and with which, the Son of God became capable to be our reconciler unto God), 'All things,' saith he, 'are delivered unto me of my Father. And all power in heaven and earth is given unto me;' and all this because he died. 'He humbled himself, and became obedient unto death, even the death of the cross; wherefore God hath highly exalted him, and given him a name above every name, that at the name of Jesus every knee should bow, of things in heaven, of things in earth, or things under the earth: and that every tongue shall confess that Jesus Christ is Lord, to the glory of God the Father' (*Phil.* 2). And all this is, as was said afore, for our sakes. He has given him to be head over all things to the church (*Eph.* 1:22).

Wherefore, whoever is set up on earth, they are set up by our Lord. 'By me,' saith he, 'kings reign, and princes decree justice. By me princes rule, and nobles, even all the judges of the earth' (*Prov.* 8:15,16). Nor are they when set up, left to do, though they should desire it, their own will and pleasure. The *Metheg-Ammah*, the bridle, (see *2 Sam.* 8:1 AV) is in his own hand, and he giveth reins, or check, even as it pleaseth him. He has this power, for the well-being of his people. Nor are the fallen angels exempted from being put under his rebuke: He is the 'only potentate' (*1 Tim.* 6:15), and in his times will show it, Peter tells us, he 'is gone into heaven, and is on the right hand of God; angels, and authorities, and powers being made subject unto him' (*1 Pet.* 3:22).

This power, as I said, he has received for the sake of his church on earth, and for her conduct and well-being among the sons of men. Hence, as he is called the king of nations, in general (*Jer.* 10:7); so the King of saints, in special (*Rev.* 15:3): and as he is said to be head *over* all things in general; so to his church in special.

e) He has given gifted ministers to his church. Another improvement that he hath made of his death for us, is, he hath obtained, and received into his own hand sufficiency of gifts to make ministers for his church withal. I say, to make and maintain, in opposition to all that would hinder, a sufficient ministry (*1 Cor.* 12:28–30). Wherefore he

[63]

saith, 'When he ascended on high, he led captivity captive, and gave gifts unto men. And he gave some apostles, some prophets, some evangelists, some pastors and teachers; for the perfecting of the saints, for the work of the ministry, for edifying of the body of Christ. Until we all come in the unity of the faith, and knowledge of the Son of God, unto a perfect man, unto the measure of the stature of the fulness of Christ' (*Eph.* 4:8–14). Many ways has Satan devised to bring into contempt this blessed advantage that Christ has received of God for the benefit of his church; partly while he stirs up persons to revile the sufficiency of the Holy Ghost, as to this thing: partly, while he stirs up his own limbs and members, to broach his delusions in the world, in the name of Christ, and as they blasphemously call it by the assistance of the Holy Ghost; partly while he tempteth novices in their faith, to study and labour in nice distinctions, and the affecting of uncouth expressions, that vary from the form of sound words, thereby to get applause, and a name, a forerunner of their own destruction (*1 Tim.* 3:6).

But, notwithstanding all this, 'Wisdom is justified of her children' (*Matt.* 11:19): and at the last day, when the *outside*, and *inside* of all things shall be seen and compared, it will appear that the Son of God has so managed his own servants in the ministry of his word, and so managed his word, while they have been labouring in it, as to put in his blessing by *that*, upon the souls of sinners, and has blown away all other things as chaff (*James* 1:18).

f) He has occupied heaven for his own. Another improvement that the Lord Christ has made of his death, for his, is the obtaining, and taking possession of heaven for them. 'By his own blood he entered in once into the holy place, having obtained eternal redemption *for us*' (*Heb.* 9:12). This heaven! who knows what it is? (*Matt.* 22:23). This glory! who knows what it is? It is called God's throne, God's house (*John* 14:2). God's habitation; paradise (*2 Cor.* 12:4), the kingdom of God, the high and holy place (*Isa.* 57:15). Abraham's bosom (*Luke* 16:22), and the place of heavenly pleasures (*Psa.* 16:11); in this heaven is to be found, *the face of God for ever* (*Psa.* 41:12). Immortality, the person of Christ, the prophets, the angels, the revelation of all mysteries, the knowledge of all the elect, ETERNITY.

Of this heaven, as was said afore, we are possessed already, we are in it, we are set down in it, and partake already of the benefits thereof, but all by our head and undertaker; and 'tis fit that we should believe this, rejoice in this, talk of this, tell one another of this, and live in the expectation of our own personal enjoyment of it. And as we should do all this, so we should bless and praise the name of God who has put this house, this kingdom, and inheritance into the hand of so faithful a friend. Yea, a brother, a Saviour and blessed undertaker for us. And lastly, since all these things already mentioned, are the fruit of the sufferings of our Jesus, and his sufferings the fruit of that love of his that *passeth knowledge*: how should we bow the knee before him, and call him tender Father; yea, how should we love and obey him, and devote ourselves unto his service, and be willing to be also sufferers for his sake, to whom be honour and glory for ever. And thus much of the love of Christ in general.

I might here add many other things, but as I told you before, we would under the head but now touched upon, treat about the fundamentals or great and chief parts thereof, [Christ's love] and so of its exceeding greatness.

II) OF ITS UNSEARCHABLENESS

Of the exceeding greatness of it more particularly: Wherefore of that we must say something now.

And to know the love of Christ, which passeth knowledge.
In that it is said to pass knowledge, 'tis manifest it is
exceeding great, or greatly going beyond what can be
known; for to exceed, is to go beyond, be above, or to be
out of the reach of what would comprehend that which is
so. And since the expression is absolutely indefinite, and
respecteth not the knowledge of *this* or the *other* creature
only: it is manifest, that Paul by his thus saying, challeng-
eth all creatures in heaven and earth to find out the
bottom of this love if they can. *The love of Christ which
passeth knowledge.* I will add, that forasmuch as he is
indefinite also about the *knowledge*, as well as about the
persons knowing, it is out of doubt that he here engageth all
knowledge, in what enlargements, attainments, improve-
ments, and heights soever it hath, or may for ever attain
unto. *It passeth knowledge* (*Eph.* 3:19).

Of the same import also is that other passage of the
apostle a little above in the self-same chapter. I preach,
saith he, among the Gentiles *the unsearchable riches of
Christ*: or those riches of Christ that cannot by searching,
be found out in the *all* of them: *The riches*, the riches of his
love and grace. The riches of his love and grace *towards us.*
'For ye know the grace of our Lord Jesus Christ, that,
though he was rich, yet for your sakes he became poor,
that ye through his poverty might be made rich'
(*2 Cor.* 8:9). Ye know the grace, that is so far, and so far
every believer knows it: for that his leaving heaven and
taking upon him flesh, that he might bring us thither, is
manifest to all. But yet, all the grace that was wrapped up
in that amazing condescension, knoweth none, nor can
know: for if that might be, that possibility would be a flat
contradiction to the text: 'The love of Christ which
passeth knowledge.' Wherefore the riches of this love in
the utmost of it, is not, cannot be known by any: let their
understanding and knowledge, be heightened and

improved what it may. Yea, and being heightened and improved, let what search there can by it be made into this love and grace. 'That which is afar off, and exceeding deep, who can find out?' (*Eccles.* 7:24). And that this love of Christ is so, shall anon be made more apparent, by showing that it surpasses:

a) The knowledge of the wisest saint

To confirm this, I need go no further than to the man that spoke these words; to wit, Paul, for in his conclusion he includes himself, saying the love of Christ which passeth knowledge, even my knowledge; though I have waded a great way in the grace of Christ, and have as much experience of his love as any in all the world, yet I confess myself short, as to the fulness that is therein, nor will I hesitate to conclude of any other, That 'he knows nothing yet as he ought to know' (*1 Cor.* 8:2; 13:12).

b) The knowledge of all the saints

Were it all put together, we, we all, and every one, did we each of us contribute for the manifesting of this love, what it is, the whole of what we know, it would amount but to a broken knowledge; we know but in part, we see darkly (*1 Cor.* 13:9–12), we walk not by sight, but faith (*2 Cor.* 5:7). This is true of saints on earth.

c) The knowledge of all the saints in heaven

But we will speak of *saints in heaven*; they cannot *to the utmost*, know this love of Christ. For though they know more thereof than saints on earth, because they are more in the open visions of it, and also are more enlarged, being spirits perfect, than we on earth. Yet, to say no more now, they do not see the rich and unsearchable runnings out thereof unto sinners here on earth. Nor may they there measure that, to others, by what they themselves knew of

[67]

it here. For sins, and times and persons and other circumstances, may much alter the case, but were all the saints on earth, and all the saints in heaven to contribute all that they know of this love of Christ, and to put it into one sum of knowledge, they would greatly come short of knowing the utmost of this love, for that there is an infinite deal of this love, yet unknown by them. 'Tis said plainly, that they on earth do not *yet* know what they shall be (*1 John* 3:2). And as for them in heaven, they are not yet made perfect *as they shall be* (*Heb.* 11:39, 40). Besides, we find the souls under the altar, how perfect now soever, when compared with that state they were in when with the body (*Isa.* 63:16); yet are not able in all points, though in glory, to know, and so to govern themselves there without directions (*Rev.* 6:9–11). I say, they are not able, without directions and instructions, to know the kinds and manner of workings of the love of Christ towards us that dwell on earth.

d) The knowledge of all the redeemed and all the angels in heaven

We will join with these, *the angels*, and when all of them, with men, have put all and every whit of what they know of this love of Christ together, they must come far short of reaching to, or of understanding the utmost bound thereof. I grant, that angels do know, in some certain parts of knowledge of the love of Christ, more than saints on earth can know while here; but then again, I know that even they do also learn many things of saints on earth, which shows that themselves know also but in part (*Eph.* 3:10); so then, *all*, as yet, as to this love of Christ, and the utmost knowledge of it, are but as so many imperfects (*1 Pet.* 1:12), nor can they all, put all their imperfects together, make up a perfect knowledge of this love of Christ; for the texts do yet stand where they did, and say, *his riches are unsearchable*, and his love that *which passeth knowledge*.

We will come now to show you, besides what has been already touched on, the reason why these riches are unsearchable and this love such as passes knowledge. The first reason is:

1) It is eternal, infinite and incomprehensible.
All that is eternal, has attending of it, as to the utmost knowledge of it, a fourfold impossibility. 1. It is without beginning. 2. It is without end. 3. It is infinite. 4. It is incomprehensible.

1. It is without beginning: That which was before the world was, is without a beginning, but the love of Christ was before the world.

This is evident from Proverbs 8:31 where, 'his delights,' before God had made the world, are said to be, 'with the sons of men.' Not that we then had being, for we were as yet uncreated; but though we had not beings created, we had being in the love and affections of Jesus Christ. Now this love of Christ must needs, as to the fulness of it, as to the utmost of it, be absolutely unknown to man. Who can tell how many heart-pleasing thoughts Christ had of us before the world began? Who can tell how much he *then* was delighted in that being we had in his affections; as also, in the consideration of our beings, believings, and being with him afterwards.

In general we may conclude, it was great; for there seems to be a parallel betwixt his Father's delights in *him*, and *his* delights in *us*. 'I was daily his delight, . . . and my delights were with the sons of men' (*Prov.* 8:22, 30, 31). But I say, who can tell, who can tell altogether, *what* and *how much* the Father delighted in his Son before the world began? Who can tell what *kind* of delight the Father had in the Son before the world began? Why there seems to be a parallel betwixt the Father's *love* to Christ, and Christ's *love* to us; the Father's *delight* in Christ, and his *delight* in us. Yea, Christ confirms it, saying, 'As the Father hath loved me, so have I loved you, continue ye in my love' (*John* 15:9). I know that I am not yet upon the nature of the word *eternal*; yet since, by eternal, we understand, before the world began, as well as forward, to an endless for-ever: We may a little enquire of folks as they may read, if they can tell the kind or measure of the love wherewith Christ then loved us. I remember the question that God asked Job, 'Where,' saith he, 'wast thou when I laid the foundation of the earth? declare if thou hast understanding' (*Job* 38:4). Thereby insinuating that because it was done before he had his being, therefore he could not tell how it was done. Now, if a work so visible, as the creation is, is yet as to the manner of the workmanship thereof wholly unknown to them that commenced in their beings afterwards: How shall that which has, in all the circumstances of it, been more hidden and inward, be found out by them that have intelligence thereof by the ear, and but in part, and that in a mystery, and long afterwards. But to conclude this, That which is eternal is without all beginning. This was presented to consideration before, and therefore it cannot to perfection be known.

2. It is without end: that which is eternal is without end, and how can an endless thing be known, that which has no end has no middle, wherefore it is impossible that the one half of the love that Christ has for his church should ever by them be known. I know that those visions that the saved shall have in heaven of this love, will far transcend our utmost knowledge here, even as far as the light of the sun at noon, goes beyond the light of a blinking candle at midnight; and hence it is, that when the days of those visions are come, the knowledge that we *now* have,

shall be swallowed up. 'When that which is perfect is come, then that which is in part shall be done away' (*1 Cor.* 13:10). And although he speaks here of perfections, 'when that which is perfect is come,' &c., yet even that perfection must not be thought to be such as is the perfection of God; for then should all that are saved be so many *eternals* and so many *infinites*, as he is infinite. But the meaning is, we shall then be with the eternal, shall immediately enjoy him with all the perfection of knowledge, as far as is possible for a creature, when he is wrought up to the utmost height that his created substance will bear to be capable of. But for all that, this perfection will yet come short of the perfection of him that made him, and consequently, short of knowing the utmost of his love; since that in the root is his very essence and nature.

I know it says also, *that we shall know even as we are known.* But yet this must not be understood, as *if* we should know God as fully as he knows us. It would be folly and madness so to conclude; but the meaning is, we are known *for* happiness; we are known of God, *for* heaven and felicity; and when that which is perfect is come, then shall we perfectly know, and enjoy that for which we are now known of God. And this is that which the Apostle longed for, namely, If by any means, he might apprehend that for which he was also apprehended of Christ Jesus (*Phil.* 3:12). That is, know, and see that, unto the which he was appointed of God and apprehended of Christ Jesus. 'Tis said again, 'We shall be like him, for we shall see him as he is' (*1 John* 3:2). This text has respect to the Son, as to his humanity, and not as to his divinity. And not as to his divinity, simply, or distinctly considered; for as to that it is as possible for a spirit to drink up the sea, as for the most enlarged saint that is, or ever shall be in glory, so to see God as to know him altogether, to the utmost, or through-out. But the humanity of the Son of God, we shall see

[71]

throughout, in all the beauty and glory that is upon him; and that was prepared for him before the foundation of the world. And Christ wills that we see this glory, when he takes us up in glory to himself (*John* 17:24); but the utmost boundlessness of the divine majesty, the eternal deity of the Son of God, cannot be known to the utmost or altogether. I do not doubt, but that there will then in him, I mean in Christ, and in us, break forth these glorious rays and beams of the eternal majesty, as will make him in each of us admirable one to another (*2 Thess.* 1:10); and that then, that of God shall be known of us, that now never entered into our hearts to think of. But the whole, is not, cannot, shall never be fully known of any. And therefore the love of Christ, it being essential to himself, cannot be known because of the endlessness that is in it.

I said before, that which has no end, has no middle, how then shall those that shall be in heaven eternally, ever pass over half the breadth of eternity? True, I know that all enjoyments there will be enjoyments eternal. Yea, that whatever we shall there embrace, or what embraces we shall be embraced with, shall be eternal; but I put a difference betwixt that which is eternal, as to the *nature*, and that which is so as to the durableness thereof. The *nature* of eternal things we shall enjoy, so soon as ever we come to heaven, but the *duration* of eternal things, them we shall never be able to pass through, for they are endless. So then, the eternal love of Christ, as to the nature of it, will be perfectly known of saints, when they shall dwell in heaven; but the endlessness thereof they shall never attain unto. And this will be their happiness. For could it be, that we should in heaven ever reach the end of our blessedness: (as we should, could we reach to the end of this love of Christ) why then, as the saying is, We should be at the land's end, and feel the bottom of all our enjoyments. Besides, whatsoever has an end, has a time to decay, and to cease to be, as well as to have a time to show forth its highest excellencies. Wherefore, from all these considerations it is most manifest, that the love of Christ is unsearchable, and that it passes knowledge.

3. and 4. It is infinite and incomprehensible. Now these other things follow of course. Wherefore here is that that still is above and beyond even those that are arrived to the utmost of their perfections. And this, if I may so say, will keep them in an employ, even when they are in heaven; though not an employ that is laboursome, tiresome, burdensome, yet an employ that is dutiful, delightful and profitable; for although the work and worship of saints in heaven is not particularly revealed as yet, and so 'it doth not yet appear what we shall be,' yet in the general we may say, there will be that for them to do, that has not yet by them been done, and by that work which they shall do there, their delight will be delight unto them. The law was the shadow and not the very image of heavenly things (*Heb.* 10:1). The image is an image, and not the heavenly things themselves (*Heb.* 9:23) which are saints and there shall be worship in the heavens. Nor will this at all derogate from their glory. The angels now wait upon God and serve him (*Psa.* 103:20); the Son of God, is now a minister, and waiteth upon his service in heaven (*Heb.* 8:1,2); some saints have been employed about service for God after they have been in heaven (*Luke* 9:29–32); and why we should be idle spectators, when we come thither, I see not reason to believe. It may be said, 'They there rest from their labours.' True, but not from their delights. All things then that once were burdensome, whether in suffering or service, shall be done away, and that which is delightful and pleasurable shall remain. *But then will be a time to receive*, and not to work. True, if by work you mean such as we now count work; but what if our work be there, to receive and bless. The fishes in the

sea do drink, swim and drink. But for a further discourse of this, let that alone till we come thither. But to come down again into the world, for now we are talking of things aloft:

II)   To know it fully means that we must fully know:

i) *All sin's nature, aggravations and tendencies*

This love of Christ must needs be beyond our knowledge, because we cannot possibly know the *utmost of our sin*. Sin is that which sets out, and off, the knowledge of the love of Christ. There are four things that must be spoken to for the clearing of this. 1. The nature of sin. 2. The aggravations of sin. 3. The utmost tendencies of sin. 4. And the perfect knowledge of all this.

1. Before we can know this love of Christ, as afore, we must necessarily know the *nature* of sin, that is, what sin is, what sin is in itself. But no man knows the nature of sin to the full; not what sin in itself is to the full. The Apostle saith, 'That sin, (that is in itself) is exceeding sinful' (*Rom.* 7:13). That is, exceeding it as to its filthiness, goes beyond our knowledge: But this is seen by the commandment. Now the reason why none can, to the full, know the horrible nature of sin, is because none, to the full, can know the blessed nature of the blessed God. For sin is the opposite to God. There is nothing that seeketh absolutely, and in its own nature to overcome, and to annihilate God, but sin, and sin doth so. Sin is worse than the devil; he therefore that is more afraid of the devil than of sin, knows not the badness of sin as he ought; nor but little of the love of Jesus Christ. He that knows not what sin would have done to the world, had not Christ stept betwixt those harms and it, how can he know so much as the extent of the love of Christ in common? And he that knows not what sin would have done to him in particular, had not Christ the Lord, stept in and saved, cannot know the utmost of the love of Christ to him in

particular. Sin therefore in the utmost evil of it, cannot be known of us: so consequently the love of Christ in the utmost goodness of it, cannot be known of us.

Besides, there are many sins committed by us, dropping from us, and that pollute us, that we are not at all aware of; how then should we know that love of Christ by which we are delivered from them? Lord, 'who can understand his errors?' said David (*Psa.* 19:12). Consequently, who can understand the love that saves him from them? moreover, he that knows the love of Christ to the full, must also know to the full that wrath and anger of God, that like hell itself, burneth against sinners for the sake of sin: but this knows none. Lord, 'who knoweth the power of thine anger?' said Moses (*Psa.* 90:11). Therefore none knows this love of Christ to the full. The nature of sin is to get into our good, to mix itself with our good, to lie lurking many times under the formality and show of good; and that so close, so cunningly, and invisibly, that the party concerned, embraces it for virtue, and knows not otherwise to do; and yet from this he is saved by the love of Christ; and therefore, as was hinted but now, if a man doth not know the nature of his wound, how should he know the nature and excellency of the balsam that hath cured him of his wound.

2. There are the due *aggravations* that belong to sin, which men are unacquainted with; it was one of the great things that the prophets were concerned with from God towards the people (*Jer.* 2) (as to show them their sins, so) to show them what aggravations did belong thereto (*Jer.* 3 and *Ezek.* 16).

There are sins against light, sins against knowledge, sins against love, sins against learning, sins against threatenings, sins against promises, vows and resolutions, sins against experience, sins against examples of anger, and sins that have great, and high, and strange aggravations attending of them; the which we are ignorant of, though not altogether, yet in too great a measure. Now if these things be so, how can the love that saveth us from them be known or understood to the full?

Alas! our ignorance of these things is manifest by our unwillingness to abide affliction, by our secret murmuring under the hand of God; by our wondering why we are so chastised as we are, by our thinking that the affliction should be sooner removed.

Or, if our ignorance of the vileness of our actions is not manifest this way, yet it is in our lightness under our guilt, our slight thoughts of our doings, our slovenly doing of duties, and asking of forgiveness after some evil or unbecoming actions. 'Tis to no boot to be particular, the whole course of our lives doth too fully make it manifest, that we are wonderful short in knowing both the nature, and also the aggravations of our sins: and how then should we know that love of Christ in its full dimensions, by which we are saved and delivered therefrom?

3. Who knows the utmost *tendencies* of sin? I mean, what the least sin driveth at, and what it would unavoidably run the sinner into. There is not a plague, a judgment, an affliction, an evil under heaven, that the least of our transgressions has not called for at the hands of the great God! nay, the least sin calleth for all the distresses that are under heaven, to fall upon the soul and body of the sinner at once. This is plain, for that the least sin deserveth hell; which is worse than all the plagues that are on earth. But I say, who understandeth this? And I say again, if one sin, the least sin deserveth all these things, what thinkest thou do all thy sins deserve? how many judgments! how many plagues! how many lashes with God's iron whip dost thou deserve? besides there is hell itself, the place itself, the fire itself, the nature of the torments, and the durableness of them, who can understand?

But this is not all, the tendencies of thy sins are to kill others. Men, good men little think how many of their neighbours one of their sins may kill. As, how many good men and good women do unawares, through their uncircumspectness, drive their own children down into the deep? (*Psa.* 106:6,7). We will easily count them very hard-hearted sinners, that used to offer their children in sacrifice to devils; when 'tis easy to do worse ourselves: they did but kill the body, but we body and soul in hell, if we have not a care.

Do we know how our sins provoke God? how they grieve the Holy Ghost? how they weaken our graces? how they spoil our prayers? how they weaken faith? how they tempt Christ to be ashamed of us? and how they hold back good from us? And if we know not every one of all these things to the full, how shall we know to the full the love of Christ which saveth us from them all?

4. Again, But who has the perfect knowledge of *all* these things? I will grant that some good souls may have waded a great way in some one, or more of them; but I know that there is not any that thoroughly know them *all*. And yet the love of Christ doth save us from *all*, notwithstanding all the vileness and soul-damning virtue that is in them. Alas! how short are we of the knowledge of ourselves, and of what is in us. How many are there that do not know that man consisteth of a body made of dust, and of an immortal soul? Yea, and how many be there of those that confess it, that know not the constitution of either. I will add, how many are there that profess themselves to be students of those two parts of man, that have oftentimes proved themselves to be but fools as to both? and I will conclude that there is not a man under heaven that knoweth it all together: For man is 'fearfully and wonderfully made' (*Psa.* 139:14): nor can the manner of the *union* of these two parts be perfectly found out. How

much more then must we needs be at loss as to the fulness of the knowledge of the love of Christ? But,

ii) All the wiles and opposition of the devil

He that altogether knoweth the love of Christ, must, precedent to that, know not only all the wiles of the devil; but also all the plottings, contrivings and designs and attempts of that wicked one; yea, he must know, all the times that he hath been with God, together with all the motions that he has made that he might have leave to fall upon us, as upon Job and Peter, to try if he might swallow us up (*Job* 1; 2; *Luke* 22:31). But who knows all this? no man, no angel. For, if the heart of man be so deep, that none, by all his actions, save God, can tell the utmost secrets that are therein; how should the heart of angels, which in all likelihood are deeper, be found out by any mortal man. And yet this must be found out before we can find out the utmost of the love of Christ to us. I conclude therefore from all these things, that the love of Christ passeth knowledge: or that by no means, the bottom, the utmost bounds thereof can be understood.

iii) All that Christ has procured by his blood

He that will presume to say, this love of Christ can be to the utmost known by us, must presume to say that he knoweth the utmost of the merits of his blood, the utmost exercise of his patience, the utmost of his intercession, the utmost of the glory that he has prepared and taken possession of for us. But I presume that there is none that can know all this, therefore I may without any fear assert, there is none that knows, that is, that knows to the full, the other.

PART THREE

Obtaining the Unsurpassable

1: *Knowing the Nature of Christ's Love*

We come now more particularly to speak of the knowledge of the love of Christ; we have spoken of the *love* of Christ; and of the *exceeding greatness* of it: and now we come, third, to speak *of the knowledge of it*; that is to say, we will show what knowledge of Christ's love is attainable in this world, under these three heads. As to this, *First*, It may be known as to the nature of it. *Second*, It may be known in many of the degrees of it. *Third*, But the greatest knowledge that we can have of it here, is to know that it passes knowledge.

(1) IN ITS NATURE WHICH IS FREE, DIVINE, HEAVENLY, EVERLASTING AND INCORRUPTIBLE

First, We may know it in the *nature* of it. That is, that it is love *free, divine, heavenly, everlasting, incorruptible*. And this no love is but the love of Christ; all other love is either love corruptible, transient, mixed, or earthly. It is *divine*, for 'tis the love of the holy nature of God. It is *heavenly*, for that it is from above: it is *everlasting*, for that it has no end: it is *immortal*, for that there is not the appearance of corruptibleness in it, or likelihood of decay.

This is general knowledge, and this is common among the saints, at leastwise in the notion of it. Though I confess, it is hard in time of temptation, practically to hold fast the soul to all these things. But, as I have said already, this love of Christ *must* be such, because love in the root of it, is essential to his nature, as also I have proved now, as is the root, such are the branches; and as is the spring, such are the streams, unless the channels in which those streams do run, should be corrupted, and so defile it; but I know no channels through which this love of Christ is conveyed unto us, but those made in his *side*, his *hands*, and his *feet*, &c. Or those gracious promises that dropped like honey from his holy lips, in the day of his love, in which he spoke them: and seeing his love is conveyed to us, as through those channels, and so by the conduit of the holy and blessed Spirit of God, to our hearts, it cannot be that it should hitherto be corrupted. I know the *cisterns*, to wit, our hearts, into which it is conveyed, are unclean, and may take away much, through the damp that they may put upon it, of the native savour and sweetness thereof. I know also, that there are those that tread down, and muddy those streams with their feet (*Ezek.* 34:18, 19); but yet neither the love nor the channels in which it runs, should bear the blame of this. And I hope those that are saints indeed, will not only be preserved to eternal life, but nourished with this that is incorruptible unto the day of Christ.

I told you before, that in the hour of temptation, it will be hard for the soul to hold fast to these things; that is, to the true definition of this love; for then, or at such seasons, it will not be admitted that the love of Christ is either transient, or mixed; but we count that we cannot be loved long, unless something better than yet we see in us, be found there, as an inducement to Christ to love, and to continue to love our poor souls (*Isa.* 64:6). But these the Christian at length gets over; for he sees, by experience, he hath no such inducement (*Deut.* 9:5); also, that Christ loves freely, and not for, or because of such poor, silly, imaginary enticements (*Ezek.* 16:60-62). Thus therefore the love of Christ may be known, that is, in the nature of it: it *may*, I say, but not easily (*Ezek.* 36:25–33). For this knowledge is neither easily got, though got, nor easily retained, though retained. There is nothing that Satan setteth himself more against, than the breaking forth of the love of Christ in its own proper *native* lustre. For he knows it destroys his kingdom, which standeth in profaneness, in errors and delusions, the only destruction of which is the knowledge of this love of Christ (*2 Cor.* 5:14). What mean those swarms of opinions that are in the world? what is the reason that some are carried about as clouds, with a tempest? what mean men's waverings, men's changing, and interchanging truth for error, and one error for another? why, this is the thing, the devil is in it. This work is his, and he makes this a-do, to make a dust; and a dust to darken the light of the gospel withal. And if he once attaineth to that, then farewell the true knowledge of the love of Christ.

Also he will assault the spirits of Christians with divers and sundry cogitations, such as shall have in them a tendency to darken the judgment, delude the fancy, to abuse the conscience. He has an art to metamorphose all things. He can make God seem to be to us, a most fierce and terrible destroyer; and Christ a terrible exactor of obedience, and most amazingly pinching of his love. He can make supposed sins unpardonable; and unpardonable ones, appear as virtues. He can make the law to be received for gospel, and cause that the gospel shall be thrown away as a fable. He can persuade, that faith is fancy, and that fancy is the best faith in the world. Besides, he can tickle the heart with false hope of a better life hereafter, even as if the love of Christ were there. But, as I said before, from all these things the true love of Christ in the right knowledge of it, delivereth those that have it shed abroad in the heart by the Holy Ghost that he hath given (*Rom.* 5). Wherefore it is for this purpose that

[83]

Christ biddeth us to *continue in his love* (*John* 15:9); because the right knowledge, and faith of that to the soul, disperseth and driveth away all such fogs, and mists of darkness; and makes the soul to sit fast in the promise of eternal life by him; yea, and to grow up into him who is the head, 'in all things.'

Before I leave this head, I will present my reader with these things, as helps to the knowledge of the love of Christ. I mean the knowledge of the *nature* of it, and as HELPS to retain it.

i) *Know oneself as a sinner*

Know thy self, what a vile, horrible, abominable sinner thou art: For thou canst not know the love of Christ, before thou knowest the badness of thy nature. 'O wretched man that I am' (*Rom.* 7:24), must be, before a man can perceive the *nature* of the love of Christ. He that sees himself *but little*, will hardly know *much* of the love of Christ: he that sees of himself *nothing at all*, will hardly ever see *anything* of the love of Christ. But he that sees *most* of what an abominable wretch he is, he is like to see *most* of what is the love of Christ. All errors in doctrine take their rise from the want of this (I mean errors in doctrine as to justification). All the idolizing of men's virtues, and human inventions, riseth also from the want of this. So then if a man would be kept sure and stedfast, let him labour before all things to know his own wretchedness. People naturally think that the knowledge of their sins is the way to destroy them; when in very deed, it is the first step to salvation. Now if thou wouldest know the badness of thy self, begin in the first place to study the law, *then* thy heart, and *so* thy life. The law thou must look into, for that's *the glass*; thy *heart* thou must look upon, for that's *the face*; thy *life* thou must look upon, for that's the *body* of a man, as to religion (*James* 1:25). And without the wary consideration of these three, 'tis not to be thought that a man can come at the knowledge of himself, and consequently to the knowledge of the love of Christ (*James* 1:26, 27).

ii) Strive to know the poverty and pollution of human righteousness

Labour to see the emptiness, shortness, and the pollution that cleaveth to a man's own righteousness. This also must in some measure be known, before a man can know the *nature* of the love of Christ. They that see nothing of the loathsomeness of man's best things, will think, that the love of Christ is of *that* nature as to be procured, or won, obtained or purchased by man's good deeds. And although so much gospel light is broken forth as to stop men's mouths from *saying* this, yet 'tis nothing else but sound conviction of the vileness of man's righteousness, that will enable men to see that the love of Christ is of that nature, as to save a man without it; as to see that it is of that nature as to justify him without it: I say, without it, or not at all. There is *shortness*, there is *hypocrisy*, there is a desire of *vain glory*, there is *pride*, there is *presumption* in man's own righteousness: nor can it be without these wickednesses, when men know not the *nature* of the love of Christ. Now these defile it, and make it abominable. Yea, if there were no imperfection in it, but that which I first did mention, to wit, *shortness*; how could it cover the nakedness of him that hath it, or obtain for the man, in whole or in part, that Christ should love, and have respect unto him.

Occasions many thou hast given thee to see the emptiness of man's own righteousness, but all will not do unless thou hast help from heaven: wherefore thy wisdom will be, if thou canst tell where to find it, to lie in the way of God, that when he comes to visit the men that wait upon him in the means of his own appointing, thou mayest be there; if perhaps he may cast an eye of pity upon thy desolate soul, and make thee see the things above-mentioned. That thou mayest know the *nature* of the love of Christ.

iii) Become familiar with the nature of the law and the nature of the gospel

If thou wouldest know the *nature* of *this* love, be much in acquainting of thy soul with the nature of the law, and the nature of the gospel (*Gal.* 3:21). The which though they are not diametrically opposite one to another, yet do propound things so differently to man, that if he knows not where, when, and how to take them, 'tis impossible but that he should confound them, and in confounding of them, lose his own soul (*Rom.* 9:31, 32). The law is a servant, both first and last, to the gospel (*Rom.* 10:3, 4): when therefore it is made a Lord, it destroyeth: and then to be sure it is made a Lord and Saviour of, when its dictates and commands are depended upon for life.

Thy wisdom therefore will be to study these things distinctly, and thoroughly; for so far as thou art ignorant of the true knowledge of the nature of these, so far thou art ignorant of the true knowledge and nature of the love of Christ. Read Paul to the Galatians, that epistle was indicted by the Holy Ghost, on purpose to direct the soul, in, and about this very thing.

iv) Keep each of these in its proper place

The right knowledge of the *nature* of the love of Christ, is obtained, and retained, by keeping of these two doctrines at an everlasting distance as to the conscience; to wit, not suffering the law to rule but over my outward man, not suffering the gospel to be removed one hair's breadth from my conscience. When Christ dwells in my heart by faith (*Eph.* 3:17), and the moral law dwells in my members

(*Col.* 3:5), the one to keep up peace with God, the other to keep my conversation in a good decorum: then am I right, and not till then.

But this will not be done without much experience, diligence, and delight in Christ. For there is nothing that Satan more desireth, than that the law may abide in the conscience of an awakened Christian, and there take up the place of Christ, and faith; for he knows if they may be obtained, the vail is presently drawn over the face of the soul, and the heart darkened as to the knowledge of Christ; and being darkened, the man is driven into despair of mercy, or is put upon it to work for life (*2 Cor.* 3:13–15). There is therefore, as I say, much diligence required of him that will keep these two in their places assigned them of God. I say much diligent study of the word, diligent prayer; with diligence to walk with God in the world. But we will pass this, and come to the second head.

2: *Knowing the Degrees of Christ's Love*

As the love of Christ may be known in the *nature* of it, so it may be known in many *degrees* of it. That which is knowable, admits of degrees of knowledge: the love of Christ is knowable. Again, that which is not possible to be known to the utmost, is to be known, we know not how much; and therefore they that seek to know it, should never be contented or satisfied to what degree of the knowledge of it soever they attain; but still should be reaching forward, because there is more to be known of it before them. 'Brethren,' said Paul, 'I count not myself to have apprehended, (that is to the utmost) but this one thing I do, forgetting those things which are behind, and reaching forth unto those things which are before, I press towards the mark for the prize of the high calling of God in Christ Jesus' (*Phil.* 3:13, 14).

I might here discourse of many things, since I am upon this head of reaching after the knowledge of the love of Christ in many of the degrees of it. But I shall content myself with few.

i) By contemplating his incarnation

He that would know the love of Christ in several degrees of it, must begin at his person, for in him *dwells* all the treasures of wisdom and knowledge. Nay, more; In him 'are hid all the treasures of wisdom and knowledge'

(*Col.* 2:3). In him, that is, in his person: For, for the godhead of Christ, and our nature to be united in one person, is the highest mystery, and the first appearance of the love of Christ by himself, to the world (*1 Tim.* 3:16). Here I say, *lie* hid the treasures of wisdom, and here, to the world, *springs* forth the riches of his love (*John* 1:14). That the eternal word, for the salvation of sinners, should come down from heaven and be made flesh, is an act of such condescension, a discovery of such love, that can never to the full be found out. Only here we may see, love in him was deep, was broad, was long, and high: let us therefore first begin here to learn to know the love of Christ, in the high degrees thereof.

a) He united our nature to God. Here, in the first place, we perceive love, in that the *human* nature, the nature of man, not of angels, is taken into union with God. Who so could consider this, as it is possible for it to be considered, would stand amazed till he died with wonder. By this very act of the heavenly wisdom, we have an unconceivable pledge of the love of Christ to man: for in that he hath taken into union with himself our *nature*, what doth it signify, but that he intendeth to take into union with himself our persons. For, for this very purpose did he assume our nature. Wherefore we read that in the flesh he took upon him, in *that* flesh, he died for us, the just for the unjust, that he might bring us to God (*1 Pet.* 3:18).

b) He was made our representative. As he was made *flesh*, so as was said afore, he became a public or common person for us: and hereby is perceived another degree of his love; undertaking to do for us, what was not possible we should do for ourselves, perfecting of righteousness to the very end of the law, and doing for us, to the reconciling of us unto his Father, and himself (*Rom.* 10:3, 4; 3:24).

c) He defeated our foes and made us conquerors. Herein also we may attain to another degree of knowledge

[89]

of his love, by understanding that he has conquered, and so disabled our foes, that they cannot now accomplish their designed enmity upon us (*Rom.* 5; *Eph.* 5:26, 27): but that when Satan, death, the grave and sin have done to his people, whatever can by them be done, we shall be still more than conquerors (though on our side be many disadvantages), through him that has loved us, over them (*Rom.* 8:37).

d) He occupied heaven for us as a forerunner. By this also we may yet see more of his love, in that as a forerunner, he is gone into heaven to take possession thereof for us (*Heb.* 6:20): there to make ready, and to prepare for us our summerhouses, our mansion, dwelling-places. As if we were the *lords*, and *he* the *servant!* (*John* 14:2, 3). Oh this love!

e) He sent the Holy Spirit to be a comforter. Also we may see another degree of his love, in this, that *now* in his absence, he has sent the third person in the Trinity to supply his place as another comforter of us (*John* 16:7; 15:26), that we may not think he has forgotten us, nor be left destitute of a revealer of truth unto us (*John* 14:16). Yea, he has sent him to fortify our spirits, and to strengthen us under all adversity; and against our enemies of what account, or degree soever (*Luke* 21:15).

f) He sympathises with his people though he is in heaven. In this also we may see yet more of the love of Christ, in that though he is in heaven and we on earth: Nothing can happen to his people to hurt them, but he *feels* it, is *touched* with it, and *counteth* it as done unto himself: Yea, *sympathises* with them, and is afflicted, and grieved in their griefs, and their afflictions.

g) He intercedes for them. Another thing by which also yet more of the love of Christ is made manifest, and so may by us be known, is this: He is now, and has been ever since his ascension into glory, laying out himself as high-priest for us (*Heb.* 7:24–26), that by the improving of his merits before the throne of grace, in way of intercession, he might preserve us from the ruins that our daily infirmities would bring upon us (*Heb.* 8:12): yea, and make our persons and performances acceptable in his Father's sight (*Rom.* 5:10; 1 *Pet.* 2:5).

h) He will bring us where he is. We also see yet more of his love by this, that he will have us where himself is, that we may behold and be partakers of his glory (*John* 17:24). And in this degree of his love, there are *many* loves.

Then he will come for us, as a bridegroom for his bride (*Matt.* 25:6–10). Then shall a public marriage be solemnised, and eternised betwixt him and his church (*Rev.* 19:6, 7). Then she shall be wrapped up in his mantles and robes of glory (*Col.* 3:4). Then they shall be separated, and separated from other sinners, and all things that offend shall be taken away from among them (*Matt.* 25:31; 13:41). Then shall they be exalted to thrones, and power of judgment; and shall also sit in judgment on sinful men and fallen angels, acquiescing, by virtue of authority, with their king and head, upon them (*1 Cor.* 6:2, 3). Then or from thenceforth for ever, there shall be no more death, sorrow, hidings of his face, or eclipsing of their glory for ever (*Luke* 20:36). And thus you may see what rungs this our Jacob's ladder hath, and how by them we may climb, and climb, even until we are climbed up to heaven: but now we are set again; for *all* the glories, *all* the benefits, *all* the blessings, and *all* the good things that are laid up in heaven for these; Who can understand?

ii) By pondering the fact that he passed by fallen angels to save us

A second thing whereby the love of Christ in *some degrees* of it may be known, is this: That he should pass by *angels* and take hold of *us*. Who so considereth the nature of spirits, as they are God's workmanship, must needs confess, that as such, they have a pre-eminency above that which is made of dust: This then was the disparity 'twixt us and them; they being, by birth, far more noble than we. But now, when both are fallen, and by our fall, both in a state of condemnation, that Jesus Christ should choose to take up us, the most inconsiderable, and pass by them, to their eternal perdition and destruction: O love! love in a high degree to man: For verily he took not hold of angels, but of the seed of Abraham he took hold (*Heb.* 2:16). Yet this is not all: In all probability this Lord Jesus has ten times as much to do now he has undertaken to be our Saviour, as he would have had, had he stepped over us and taken hold on them.

a) He would not have needed to stoop so low to save angels as humans. He needed not to have stooped so low as to take flesh upon him; theirs being a more noble nature.

b) They probably would have recognised him and responded better than we. Nor would he in all likelihood, have met with those contempts, those scorns, those reproaches and undervaluings from them, as he has all-along received in this his undertaking, and met with from sinful flesh. For they were more noble than we, and would sooner have perceived the design of grace, and so one would think more readily have fallen in therewith, than [creatures in] such darkness as we were, and still by sin are.

c) Had God chosen them, we would not have been able to hinder their faith and hope, as they do ours. They would not have had those disadvantages as we, for that they would not have had a tempter, a destroyer, so strong and mighty as ours is. Alas! had God left us, and taken them, though we should have been ever so full of envy against their salvation; yet being but flesh, what could we have done to them to have laid obstacles in the way of their faith and hope, as they can and do in ours?

d) They would probably have dealt with remaining sin more easily than we. They, it may fairly be presumed, had they been taken, and we left, and made partakers in our stead, while we had been shut out, as they are, would not have put Christ so to it, now in heaven (pray bear with the expression, because I want a better) as we by our imperfections have done and do. Sin, methinks, would not have so hanged in their natures as it doth in ours: their reason, and sense, and apprehensions being more quick, and so more apt to have been taken with this love of Christ, and by it more easily have been sanctified.

e) They would probably have kept the law more fully and promptly. The law which they have broken, being not so intricate, as that against which we have offended, theirs being a commandment with faithfulness to abide in the place in which their Creator had set them; methinks, considering also the aptness of their natures as angels, would not have made their complete obedience so difficult.

f) They would have praised God more worthily than we. Nor can I imagine, but had they been taken, they, as creatures excelling in strength, would have been more capable of rendering these praises and blessings to God for eternal mercies, than such poor sorry creatures as we are, could. But! 'behold what manner of love the Father hath bestowed upon us, that we should be called the children of God' (*1 John* 3:1). That *we*, not they, that *we* notwithstanding all that they have, or could have done to hinder it, should be called the children of God.

This therefore is an high degree of the love of Jesus Christ to us, that when we and they were fallen, he should stoop and take up us, the more ignoble, and leave so mighty a creature in his sins to perish.

iii) By pondering the effort involved to bring sinners to glory

A third thing whereby the love of Christ in *some* of the degrees of it may be known, will be to consider more particularly the way, and unwearied work that he hath with man to bring him to that kingdom, that by his blood he hath obtained for him.

a) They are at enmity against him. Man, when the Lord Jesus takes him in hand to make him partaker of the benefit, is found an enemy to his redeemer; nor doth all the intelligence that he has had of the grace and love of Christ to such, mollify him at all, to wit, before the day of God's power comes (*Rom.* 4:5; 5:7–10). And this is a strange thing. Had man, though he could not have come to Christ, been willing that Christ should have come to him, it had been something; it would have shown that he had taken his grace to heart, and considered of it: yea, and that he was willing to be a sharer in it. But verily here is no such thing; man, though he has free will, yet is willing by no means to be saved God's way, to wit, by Jesus Christ, before (as was said before) the day of God's power comes upon him. When the good shepherd went to look for his sheep that was lost in the wilderness, and had found it: did it go one step homewards upon its own legs? did not the shepherd take her and lay her upon his shoulder, and bring her home rejoicing (*Luke* 15)? This then is not love only, but love to a degree.

b) They are averse to being taught by him. When man is taken, and laid under the day of God's power: When Christ is opening his ear to discipline, and speaking to him that his heart may receive instruction; many times that poor man is, as if the devil had found him, and not God. How frenziedly he imagines! how crossly he thinks! How ungainly he carries it under convictions, counsels, and his present apprehension of things! I know some are more powerfully dealt withal, and more strongly bound at first by the world; but others more in an ordinary manner, that the flesh, and reason may be seen, to the glory of Christ. Yea, and where the will is made more quickly to comply with its salvation, 'tis no thanks to the sinner at all (*Job* 4:18). 'Tis the day of the power of the Lord that has made the work so soon to appear. Therefore count this an act of love, *in the height of love*; Love in a great degree (*John* 15:16).

c) They are prone to wander from him. When Christ Jesus has made this mad man to come to himself, and persuaded him to be willing to accept of his salvation: yet he may not be trusted, nor left alone, for then the corruptions that still lie scattering up and down in his flesh will tempt him to it, and he will be gone; yea, so desperately wicked is the flesh of saints, that should they be left to themselves but a little while, none knows what horrible transgressions would break out. Proof of this we have to amazement, plentifully scattered here and there in the word. Hence we have the patience of God, and his gentleness so admired (*2 Chron.* 32:21): for through that it is that they are preserved. He that keepeth Israel neither slumbers nor sleeps (*Psa.* 121:4), but watches for them, and over them every moment, for he knows else they will be hurt (*Isa.* 27:3).

d) They sin openly and refuse to confess it. Yea, notwithstanding this, how often are saints found playing *truant*, and lurking like thieves in one hole or other. Now, in the guilt of backsliding by the power of this, and then in filth by the power of that corruption (*Jer.* 2:26). Yea, and when found in such decayings, and under such revoltings from God, how commonly do they hide their sin with Adam, and David, even until their Saviour fireth out of their mouths a confession of the truth of their naughtiness. 'When I kept silence,' said David (and yet he chose to keep silence after he had committed his wickedness),

[95]

'my bones waxed old through my roaring all the day long. For day and night thy hand was heavy upon me, my moisture is turned into the drought of summer' (*Psa.* 32:3, 4). But why didst thou not confess what thou hadst done *then?* So I did, saith he, at last, and thou forgavest the iniquity of my sin (verse 5).

e) He chastises them instead of destroying them. When the sins of saints are so visible and apparent to others, that God for the vindication of his name and honour must punish them in the sight of others; yea, must do it, as he is just: Yet then for Christ's sake, he waveth such judgments, and refuseth to inflict such punishments as naturally tend to their destruction, and chooseth to chastise them with such rods and scourges, as may do them good in the end; and that they may not be condemned with the world (*1 Cor.* 11:31, 32). Wherefore the Lord loves them, and they are blessed, whom he chasteneth and teacheth out of his law (*Heb.* 12:5-8 and *Psa.* 94:12). And these things are love to a degree.

f) He preserves his work in their hearts. That Christ should supply out of his fulness the beginnings of grace in our souls, and carry on that work of so great concern, and that which at times we have so little esteem of, is none of the least of the aggravations of the love of Christ to his people. And this work is as common as any of the works of Christ, and as *necessary* to our *salvation*, as is his righteousness, and the *imputation thereof* to our *justification*: For else how could we hold out to the end (*Matt.* 24:13); and yet none else can be saved.

g) He loves them more and more. And that the love of Christ should be such to us that he will thus act, thus do to, and for us, with gladness; (as afore is manifest by the parable of the lost sheep) is another degree of his love towards us: And such an one too, as is none of the lowest rate. I have seen hot love, soon cold; and love that has continued to act, yet act towards the end, as the man that by running, and has run himself off his legs, *pants*, and can hardly run any longer: but I never saw love like the love of Christ, who as a giant, and bridegroom coming out of his chamber, and as a strong man, *rejoiceth to run his race* (*Psa.* 19:5). Loving higher and higher, stronger and stronger, I mean as to the lettings out of love, for he reserveth the best wine even till the last (*John* 2:10).

h) He delights most in loving the worst. I will conclude with this, that his love may be known in many degrees of it, by that sort of sinners whose salvation he *most* rejoiceth in, and that is, in the salvation of the sinners that are of the biggest size: Great sinners, *Jerusalem* sinners, *Samaritan* sinners, publican sinners. I might urge moreover, how he hath proportioned invitations, promises and examples of his love, for the encouragement and support of those whose souls would trust in him: By which also great degrees of his love may be understood. But we will come now to the third thing that was propounded.

3: *Knowing the Mystery of Christ's Love*

But the greatest attainment, that as to the understanding of the love of Christ, we can arrive to here, is to *know* that it passes *knowledge*: *And to know the love of Christ that passeth knowledge.* This truth discovereth itself,

i) The statement in the text itself

By the text itself, for the apostle here, in this prayer of his for the Ephesians, doth not only desire that they may know, but describeth that thing which he prays they may know, by this term, *It passeth knowledge.* And to know the love of Christ which passeth knowledge. As our reason and carnal imagination will be rudely, and unduly tampering with any thing of Christ, so more especially with the love and kindness of Christ: Judging and concluding that just such it is, and none other, as may be apprehended by them; Yea, and will have a belief that just so, and no otherwise are the dimensions of this love; nor can it save beyond our carnal conceptions of it. Saying to the soul as Pharaoh once did to Israel in another case: 'Let the Lord be with you as I shall' (judge it meet he should) 'let you go.' We think Christ loves us no more than *we* do think he can, and so conclude that his love is such as may by us be comprehended, or known to the utmost bounds thereof. But these are false conceptions, and this love of Christ that we think is such, is indeed none of the love of Christ, but a false image thereof, set before our eyes. I speak not now of weak knowledge, but of foolish and bold conclusions. A man through unbelief may think that Christ has no love for him, and yet Christ may love him with a love that passeth knowledge. But when men in the common course of their profession, will be always terminating here, that they know how, and how far Christ can love, and will thence be bold to conclude of their own safety, and of the loss and ruin of all that are not in the same notions, opinions, formalities, or judgments as they: this is the worst and greatest of all. The text therefore, to rectify those false and erroneous conclusions, says, *It is a love that passeth knowledge.*

And it will be worth our observation to take notice that men, erroneous men, do not put these limits so commonly to the Father and his love, as [to] the Son and his. Hence you have some that boast that God can save some who have not the knowledge of the person of the mediator Jesus Christ the righteous; as the heathens that have, and still do make a great improvement of the law and light of nature: crying out with disdain against the narrowness, rigidness, censoriousness, and pride of those that think the contrary. Being not ashamed all the while to eclipse, to degrade, to lessen and undervalue the love of Jesus Christ; making of him and his undertakings, to offer himself a sacrifice to appease the justice of God for our sins, but a thing indifferent, and in its own nature but as other smaller matters.

But all this while the devil knows full well at what game he plays, for he knows that without Christ, without faith in his blood, there is no remission of sins. Wherefore, saith he, let these men talk what they will of the greatness of the love of God as *creator*, so they slight and undervalue the love of Christ as *mediator*. And yet it is worth our consideration, that the greatness of the love of God is most expressed in his giving of Christ to be a Saviour, and in bestowing his benefits upon us that we may be happy through him.

But to return, The love of Christ that is so indeed, is love that passeth knowledge: and the best and highest of our knowledge of it is, that we know it to be such.

ii) The examples of great men of God

Because I find that at this point, the *great men of God*, of old, were wont to stop, be set, and beyond which they could not pass. 'Twas this that made Moses wonder (*Deut.* 4:31–34). 'Twas this that made David cry out, How great and wonderful are the works of God? 'Thy thoughts to usward: they cannot be reckoned up in order unto thee: If I would declare and speak of them, they are more than can be numbered' (*Psa.* 40:5). And again, 'How precious also are thy thoughts unto me, O God! how great is the sum of them! If I should count them, they are more in number than the sand' (*Psa.* 139:17, 18). And a little before, '*such* knowledge *is* too wonderful for me' (verse 6). Isaiah saith, there hath not entered into the heart of man what God has prepared for them that wait for him (*Isa.* 64:4). Ezekiel says, this is the river that cannot be passed over (47:5): And Micah to the sea (7:19), and Zechariah to a fountain, hath compared this unsearchable love (13:1). Wherefore the Apostle's position, *That the love of Christ is that which passeth knowledge*, is a truth not to be doubted of: Consequently, to know this, *and that it is such*, is the farthest that we can go. This is to justify God, who has said it, and to magnify the Son, who has loved us with such a love: And the contrary is to dishonour him, to lessen him, and to make him a *deficient* Saviour. For suppose this should be true, that thou couldest to the utmost comprehend this love; yet unless, by thy knowledge thou canst comprehend beyond all evil of sin, or beyond what any man's sins, who shall be saved, can spread themselves or infect: Thou must leave some pardonable man in an unpardonable condition. For that thou canst comprehend this love, and yet canst not comprehend that sin. This makes Christ a deficient Saviour. Besides, if thou comprehendest truly; the word that says, it passeth knowledge, hast lost its sanctity, its truth.

It must therefore be, that this love passeth knowledge; and that the highest pitch that a man by knowledge can attain unto, as to this, is to *know* that *it passeth knowledge*. My reason is, for that all degrees of love, be they never so high, or many, and high, yet, if we can comprehend them, rest in the bowels of our knowledge, for that only which is beyond us, is that which passeth knowledge. That which we can reach, cannot be the highest: And if a man thinks there is nothing beyond what he can reach, he has no more knowledge as to that: but if he knows that together with what he hath already reached, there is that which he cannot reach, before [him]; then he has a knowledge for that also, even a knowledge, that it *passeth* knowledge. 'Tis true a man that thus knoweth may have divers conjectures about that thing that is beyond his knowledge. Yea, in reason it will be so, because he knows that there is something yet before him: But since the thing itself is truly beyond his knowledge, none of his conjectures about that thing may be counted knowledge. Or suppose a man that thus conjectureth, should hit right as to what he now conjectures; his right hitting about that thing may not be called *knowledge*: It is as yet *to him* but as an uncertain guess, and is still beyond his knowledge.

iii) *The advantages of knowing in part*

Question. But, may some say, what good will it do a man to know that the love of Christ passeth knowledge? one would think that it should do one more good to believe that the knowledge of the whole love of Christ might be attainable.

Answer. That there is an advantage in knowing that the love of Christ passeth knowledge; must not be questioned, for that the Apostle saith it doth (*2 Tim.* 3:16). For to *know* what the holy word affirms, is profitable: nor would he pray that we might *know* that which passeth *knowledge*, were there not by our knowing of it, some help to be administered. But to shew you some of the advantages that will come to us by knowing that the love of Christ passeth knowledge.

a) It is a means of recovery from a time of temptation. By knowing of this a child of God has in *reserve* for himself, at a day, when all that he otherwise knows, may be taken from him through the power of temptation. Sometimes a good man may be so put to it, that all that he knows comprehensively, may be taken from him: to wit, the knowledge of the truth of his faith, or that he has the grace of God in him, or the like, this I say may be taken from him. Now if at this time, *he knows the love of Christ that passeth knowledge*, he knows a way in all probability to be recovered again. For if Christ Jesus loves with a love that passeth knowledge: then, saith the soul, that is thus in the dark, he may love me yet, for ought I know, for I know that he loves with a love that passeth knowledge; and therefore I will not utterly despond. Yea, if Satan should attempt to question whether ever Christ Jesus will look upon me or no: the answer is, if I know the love that passes knowledge: But he may look upon me, (O, Satan) yea, and love, and save me too, for ought I poor sinner know; for he loves with a love that passeth knowledge. If I be fallen into sin that lies hard upon me, and my conscience fears, that for this there is no forgiveness. The help for a stay from utter despair is at hand: but there may, say I, for Christ loves, with a love that passeth knowledge. If Satan would dissuade me from praying to God, by suggesting as if Christ would not regard the stammering, and chattering prayer of mine. The answer is ready, but he may regard for aught I know; for he loves with a love that passeth knowledge. If the tempter doth suggest that thy trials, and troubles, and afflictions, are so many, that it is to be thought thou shall never get beyond them. The answer is near, but for aught we know, Christ may carry me through them all, for he loves with a love that passeth knowledge. Thus I say, is relief at hand, and a help in reserve for the tempted, let their temptations be what they will. This therefore is the weapon that will baffle the devil when all other weapons fail; for aught I know, Christ may save me, for he loves with a love that passeth knowledge. Yea, suppose he should drive me to the worst of fears, and that is to doubt that I neither have nor shall have for ever the grace of God in my soul. The answer is at hand, but I have or may have it, for Christ loves with a love that passeth knowledge. Thus therefore you may see that in this prayer of Paul, there is a great deal of good. He prays, when he prays that we might know the love of Christ that passeth knowledge: that we may have a help at hand, and relief against all the horrible temptations of the devil. For this is a help at hand, a help that is ready to fall in with us, if there be yet remaining with us, but the least grain of right reasoning according to the nature of things. For if it be objected against a man that he is poor, because he has but a groat in his pocket; yet if he has an unknown deal of money in his trunks, how easy is it for him to recover himself from that slander, by returning the knowledge of what he has, upon the objector. This is the case, and thus is is, and will be with them that know the love of Christ that passeth knowledge. Wherefore,

b) It is a resource for Christian living in a time of difficulty. By this knowledge, room is made for a Christian, and liberty is ministered unto him, to turn himself every way in all spiritual things. This is the Christian's

Rehoboth, that well for which the Philistines have no heart to strive, and that which will cause that we be fruitful in the land (*Gen.* 26:22).

If Christians know not with this knowledge, they walk in the world as if they were *pinioned*; or as if fetters were hanged on their heels. But this enlarges their steps under them (*2 Sam.* 22:37): by the knowledge of *this* love they may walk at liberty, and their steps shall not be straitened. This is that which Solomon intends when he saith, 'Get wisdom, and get understanding' (*Prov.* 4:5). Then 'when thou goest, thy steps shall not be straitened, and when thou runnest, thou shalt not stumble' (*Prov.* 4:12). A man that has only from hand to mouth, is oft put to it to know how to use his penny, and comes off also, many times, but with an hungry belly; but he that has, not only that, but always over and to spare, he is more at liberty, and can live in fulness, and far more like a gentleman. There is a man has a cistern, and that is full of water: there is another also, that has his cistern full, and withal, his spring in his yard; but a great drought is upon the land in which they dwell: I would now know, which of these two have the most advantage to live in their own minds at liberty, without fear of wanting water? Why this is the case in hand. There is a Christian that knows Christ in all those degrees of his love that are knowable, but he knoweth Christ nothing in his love that passeth knowledge. There is another Christian, and he knows Christ, as the first, but withal, he also knows him as to his love that passeth knowledge. Pray now tell me, which of these two are likeliest to live most like a Christian, that is, like a spiritual prince, and like him that possesseth all things? which has most advantage to live in godly largeness of heart, and is most at liberty in his mind? which of these two have the greatest advantage to believe, and the greatest engagements laid upon him to love the Lord Jesus? which of these have also most in readiness to resist the wiles of the devil, and to subdue the power and prevalency of corruptions? 'Tis *this*, that makes men fathers in Christianity. 'I write unto you, fathers, because ye have known; . . . I have written unto you, fathers, because ye have known' (*1 John* 2:13–14), why, have not others known, not so as the fathers? The fathers have *known* and *known*. They have known the love of Christ in those degrees of love which are *knowable*, and have also known the love of Christ to be such which *passeth knowledge*. In my father's house is bread enough and to spare, was that that fetched the prodigal home (*Luke* 15:17). And when Moses would speak an endless all to Israel, for the comfort and stay of their souls, he calls their God, 'The fountain of Jacob upon a land of corn and wine' (*Deut.* 33:28).

c) It promotes a desire to press forward to glory. By this knowledge, or knowing of the love of Christ which passeth knowledge, there is begotten in Christians a greater desire to press forwards to that which is before them (*Phil.* 3:12–21). What is the reason for all that sloth, carnal contentedness, and listlessness of spirit in Christians, more than the ignorance of this. For he that thinks he *knows* what can be *known*, is beyond all reason that should induce him to seek yet after more. Now the love of Christ may be said, not to be *knowable*, upon a threefold account: [namely.] For that my knowledge is *weak*. For that my knowledge is *imperfect*. Or for that, though my knowledge be never so perfect, because the love of Christ is *eternal*.

There is love that is not to be apprehended by weak knowledge. Convince a man of this, and then, if the knowledge of what he already has, be truly sweet to this soul (*Prov.* 2:10), it will stir him up with great heartiness to desire to know what more of this is possible.

There is love beyond what he knows already, who is indued with the most perfect knowledge, that man here may have. Now if what this man knows already of this love is indeed sweet unto him; then it puts him upon hearty desires that his soul may yet know more. And because there is no bound set to man, how much he may *know* in this life thereof; therefore his desires, notwithstanding what he has attained, are yet *kept alive*, and in the pursuit after the knowledge of more of the love of Christ. And God in old time has taken it so well at the hands of some of his, that their desires have been so great, that when, as I may say, they have known as much on earth as is possible for them to know; (that is by ordinary means) he has come down to them in visions and revelations; or else taken them up to him for an hour or two into paradise, that they might *know*, and then let them down again.

But this is not all, There is a knowledge of the love of Christ, that we are by no means capable of until we be possessed of the heavens. And I would know, if a man indeed loveth Christ, whether the belief of this be not one of the highest arguments that can be urged, to make such an one weary of this world, that he may be with him. To such an one, 'to live is Christ, and to die is gain' (*Phil.* 1:21-23). And to such an one, it is difficult to bring his mind to be content to stay here a longer time; except he be satisfied that Christ has still work for him here to do.

I will yet add, There is a love of Christ, I will not say, that cannot be *known*, but I will say, that cannot be *enjoyed*; no, not by them now in heaven (in soul) until the day of judgment. And the knowledge of this, when it has possessed even men on earth, has made them choose a day of judgment, before a day of death, that they might know what is beyond that state and knowledge which even the spirits of just men made perfect, now do enjoy in heaven (*2 Cor.* 5:4). Wherefore, as I said at first, *To know the love of Christ that passeth knowledge*, is advantageous upon this account; it begetteth in Christians a great desire to reach, and press forward to that which is before.

One thing more, and then, as to this reason, I have done. Even that love of Christ that is absolutely unknowable, as to the utmost bound thereof because it is eternal, will be yet in the *nature* of it sweet and desirable, because we shall enjoy or be possessed of it *so*. This therefore, if there were no more, is enough, when known, to draw away the heart from things that are below, to itself.

d) It leads to being 'filled with the fulness of God'. The *love that passeth knowledge*. The knowledge of that is a very fruitful knowledge. It cannot be, but it must be fruitful. Some knowledge is empty, and alone, not attended with that good, and with those blessings wherewith this knowledge is attended. Did I say, it is fruitful? I will add, it is attended with the best fruit; it yieldeth the best wine: It fills the soul with all the fulness of God. '*And to know the love of Christ which passeth knowledge*, that ye may be filled with all the fulness of God.' God is in Christ, and makes himself known to us by the love of Christ. 'Whosoever transgresseth, and abideth not in the doctrine of Christ, hath not God,' for God is not to be found nor enjoyed, but in him, consequently, he that hath, and abideth in the doctrine of Christ, 'hath both the Father and the Son' (*2 John* 9). Now, since there are degrees of knowledge of this doctrine, and since the highest degree of the knowledge of him, is to know that he has a *Love that passeth knowledge*, it follows, that if he that has the least saving knowledge of this doctrine, hath God; he that hath the largest knowledge of it, has God much more, or, according to the text, is filled with all the fulness of God. What this fulness of God should be, is best gathered from such sayings of the Holy Ghost, as come nearest to this, in language, filled,

Full of goodness (*Rom.* 15:14).

Full of faith (*Acts* 6:5).

Full of the Holy Ghost (*Acts* 7:55).

Full of assurance of faith (*Heb.* 10:22).

Full of assurance of hope (*Heb.* 6:11).

Full of joy unspeakable, and full of glory (*1 Pet.* 1:8).

Full of joy (*1 John* 1:4).

Full of good works (*Acts* 11:36).

Being filled with the knowledge of his will (*Col.* 1:9).

Being filled with the spirit (*Eph.* 5:18).

Filled with the fruits of righteousness, which are by Jesus Christ unto the glory and praise of God (*Phil.* 4:11).

These things to be sure are included either for the cause or effect of this *fulness*. The cause they cannot be, for that is God's, by his Holy Spirit. The effects therefore they are, for wherever God dwells in the degree intended in the text, there is shown in an eminent manner, by these things, 'what *is* the riches of the glory of his inheritance in the saints' (*Eph.* 1:18). But these things dwell not in that measure specified by the text, in any, but those who *know the love of Christ which passeth knowledge*.

But what a man is he that is filled with all these things! or that is, as we have it in the text, 'filled with all the fulness of God!' Such men are, at this day, wanting in the churches. These are the men that *sweeten* churches, and that bring glory to God and to religion. And knowledge will make us such, such *knowledge* as the Apostle here speaketh of.

PART FOUR

Uses and Counsels

1: *See the Greatness of God's Good Will to Believers!*

I have now done, when I have spoken something by way of USE unto you, from what hath been said. And,

Is there such breadth, and length, and depth, and height in God, for us? And is there toward us love in Christ that passeth knowledge? Then this shews us, not only the greatness of the majesty of the Father and the Son, but the great good will that is in their heart to them that receive their word.

God has engaged the breadth, and length and depth, and height of the love, the wisdom, the power, and truth that is in himself, for us; and Christ has loved us with a love that passeth knowledge. We may well say, 'Who is like thee, O Lord, among the gods?' (*Exod.* 15:11). Or, as another prophet has it, 'Who is a God like unto thee, that pardoneth iniquity, and passeth by the transgression of the remnant of his heritage? he retaineth not his anger for ever: because he delighteth in mercy' (*Micah* 7:18). Yea, no words can sufficiently set forth the greatness of this love of God and his Son to us poor miserable sinners.

2: The Message of this Good Will to Believers

(1) IT CALLS BELIEVERS:

i) To ponder and search after it.

Is there so great a heart for love, towards us, both in the Father and in the Son? Then let us be much in the study and search after the greatness of this love. This is the sweetest study that a man can devote himself unto; because it is the study of the love of God and of Christ to man. Studies that yield far less profit than this, how close are they pursued, by some who have adapted themselves thereunto? Men do not use to count telling over of their money burdensome to them, nor yet the recounting of their grounds, their herds, and their flocks, when they increase. Why? the study of the unsearchable love of God in Christ to man, is better in itself, and yields more sweetness to the soul of man, than can ten thousand such things as but now are mentioned. I know the wise men of this world, of whom there are many, will say as to what I now press you unto; 'Who can shew us any good in it? But Lord, lift thou up the light of thy countenance upon us. Thou hast put gladness in my heart, more than in the time that their corn and their wine increaseth' (*Psa.* 4:6, 7). David also said that his meditation on the Lord should be sweet. Oh, there is in God and in his Son, that kindness for the sons of men, that, did they know it, they would like to retain the knowledge of it in their hearts. They would cry out as she did of old; 'Set me as a seal upon thy heart, as a seal upon thine arm: For love is strong as death' (*Song of Sol.* 8:6, 7). Every part, crumb, grain, or scrap of this knowledge, is to a Christian, as drops of honey are to sweet-palated children, worth the gathering up, worth the putting to the taste to be relished. Yea, David says of the word which is the ground of knowledge: 'It is sweeter than honey or the honey-comb. More,' saith he, 'to be desired are they than gold; yea, than much fine gold; sweeter also than honey or the honey-comb' (*Psa.* 19:10). Why then do not Christians devote themselves to the meditation of this so heavenly, so goodly, so sweet, and so comfortable a thing, that yieldeth such advantage to the soul? The reason is, these things are talked of, but not believed: did men believe what they say, when they speak so largely of the love of God, and the love of Jesus Christ, they would, they could not but meditate upon it. There are so many wonders in it, and men love to think of wonders. There is so much profit in it, and men love to think of that which yields them profit. But, as I said, the belief of things is wanting. Belief of a thing will have strong effects, whether the ground for it be true, or false. As suppose one of you should, when you are at a neighbour's house, believe that your own house is on fire, whilst your children are fast asleep in bed, though indeed there were no such thing; I will appeal to any of you if this belief would not make notable work with and upon your hearts. Let a man believe he shall be damned, though afterwards it is evident he believed a lie, yet what work did that belief make in that man's heart; even so, and much more, the belief of heavenly things will work, because true and great, and most good; also, where they are indeed believed, their evidence is managed upon their spirit, by the power and glory of the Holy Ghost himself: Wherefore let us study these things.

ii) To cast themselves on it

Let us cast ourselves upon this love. No greater encouragement can be given us, than what is in the text and about it. It is great, it is love that passeth knowledge. Men that are sensible of danger, are glad when they hear of such helps upon which they may boldly venture for escape. Why such an help and relief, the text helpeth trembling and fearful consciences to. Fear and trembling as to misery hereafter, can flow but from what we know, feel, or imagine: but the text speaks of a love that is beyond what we can know, feel, or imagine, even of a love that passeth knowledge; consequently of a love that goes beyond all these. Besides, the Apostle's conclusion upon this subject, plainly makes it manifest that this meaning which I have put upon the text, is the mind of the Holy Ghost. 'Now unto him,' saith he, 'that is able to do exceeding abundantly above all that we ask or think, according to the power that worketh in us, unto him be glory in the church by Christ Jesus, throughout all ages, world without end. Amen' (*Eph.* 3:20, 21). What can be more plain? what can be more full? What can be more suitable to the most desponding spirit in any man? He can do more than thou knowest he will. He can do more than thou thinkest he can.

What dost thou think? why, I think, saith the sinner, *that I am cast away.* Well, but there are worse thoughts than these, therefore think again. Why, saith the sinner, *I think that my sins are as many as the sins of all the world.* Indeed this is a very black thought, but there are worse thoughts than this, therefore prithee think again. Why, *I think,* saith the sinner, *that God is not able to pardon all my sins.* Ay, now thou hast thought indeed. For this thought makes thee look more like a devil than a man, and yet because thou art a man and not a devil, see the condescension and the boundlessness of the love of thy God. *He is able to do above all that we think!* Couldest thou (sinner) if thou hadst been allowed, thyself express what thou wouldest have expressed, the greatness of the love thou wantest, with words that could have suited thee better? for 'tis not said he can do above what we think, meaning our thinking at present, but above all we can think, meaning above the worst and most soul-dejecting thoughts that we have at any time. Sometimes the dejected have worse thoughts than at other times they have. Well, take them at their worst times, at times when they think, and think, till they think themselves down into the very pangs of hell; yet this word of the grace of God, is above them, and shows that he can yet recover and save this miserable people.

And now I am upon this subject, I will a little further walk and travel with the desponding ones, and will put a few words in their mouths for their help against temptations that may come upon them hereafter. For as Satan follows such now, with charges and applications of guilt, so he may follow them with interrogatories and appeals: for he can tell how by appeals, as well as by charging of sin, to sink and drown the sinner whose soul he has leave to engage. Suppose therefore that some distressed man or woman, should after this way be engaged, and Satan should with his interrogatories, and appeals be busy with them to drive them to desperation; the text last mentioned, to say nothing of the subject of our discourse, yields plenty of help for the relief of such a one. Says Satan, dost thou not know that thou hast horribly sinned? yes, says the soul, I do. Says Satan, dost thou not know, that thou art one of the vilest in all the pack of professors? yes, says the soul, I do. Says Satan, doth not thy conscience tell thee that thou art and hast been more base than any of thy fellows can imagine thee to be? Yes, says the soul; my conscience tells me so. Well, saith Satan, now will I come upon thee with my appeals. Art thou not a graceless wretch? Yes. Hast thou an heart to be sorry for this wickedness? No, not as I should. And albeit, saith Satan, thou prayest sometimes, yet is not thy heart possessed with a belief that God will not regard thee? yes, says the sinner. Why then despair, and go hang thyself, saith the devil. And now we are at the end of the thing designed and driven at by Satan. But what shall I now do, saith the sinner; I answer, take up the words of the text against him, Christ loves with a love that passeth knowledge, and answereth him farther, saying Satan, though I cannot think that God loves me; yet I will not yield to thee: for God can do more than I think he can. And whereas thou appealedst unto me, if whether when I pray, my heart is not possessed with unbelief that God will not regard me; that shall not sink me neither: for God can do abundantly above what I ask or think. Thus this text helpeth, where obstructions are put in against our believing, and thereby casting ourselves upon the love of God in Christ for salvation.

And yet this is not all, for the text is yet more full: 'He is able to do abundantly more,' yea, 'exceeding abundantly more,' or 'above all that we ask or think.' It is a text made up of words *picked* and *packed* together by the wisdom of God, *picked* and *packed* together on purpose for the succour and relief of the tempted, that they may when in the midst of their distresses, cast themselves upon the Lord their God. He can do abundantly more than we *ask*. Oh! says the soul, that he would but do *so* much for me as I could *ask* him to do! How happy a man should I then be. Why, what wouldest thou *ask* for, sinner? you may be sure, says the soul, I would ask *to be saved* from my sins; I would ask for *faith* in, and *love* to, Christ; I would ask to be preserved in this evil world, and ask to be glorified with Christ in heaven. He that *asketh* for all this, doth indeed *ask* for much, and for more than Satan would have him believe that God is able or willing to bestow upon him; but mark, the text doth not say, that God is able to do *all* that we can *ask or think*, but that he is able to do *above* all, yea, *abundantly* above all, yea, *exceeding* abundantly above all that we ask or think. What a text is this! What a God have we! God foresaw the sins of his people, and what work the devil would make with their hearts about them, and therefore to prevent their ruin by his temptation, he has thus largely, as you see, expressed his love by his word. Let us therefore, as has been bidden us, make this good use of this doctrine of grace, as to cast ourselves upon this love of God in the times of distress and temptation.

iii) To take heed of abusing it.
Take heed of abusing this love. This exhortation seems needless; for love is such a thing, that one would think none could find in their heart to abuse. But for all that, I am of opinion, that there is nothing that is more abused among professors this day, than is this love of God. There has of late more light about the love of Christ broken out, than formerly: every boy now can *talk* of the love of Christ; but this love of Christ has not been rightly applied by preachers, or else not rightly received by professors. For never was this grace of Christ so turned into lasciviousness, as now. Now it is a practice among professors to learn to be vile, of the profane. Yea, and to plead for that vileness: Nay, we will turn it the other way, now it is so that the profane do learn to be vile of those that profess (They teach the wicked ones their ways:) (*Jer.* 2:33): a thing that no good man should think on but with blushing cheeks.

Jude speaketh of these people, and tells us that they, notwithstanding their profession, deny the only Lord God, and our Saviour Jesus Christ (verse 4). 'They profess,' saith Paul, 'that they know God; but in works they deny *him*, being abominable, and disobedient, and unto every good work reprobate' (*Titus* 1:16).

But I say, let not this love of God and of Christ, be abused. 'Tis unnatural to abuse love, to abuse love is a villany condemned of all, yea, to abuse love, is the most inexcusable sin of all. It is next the sin of devils to abuse love, the love of God and of Christ.

And what says the Apostle? 'Because they received not the love of the truth, that they might be saved, therefore God shall send them strong delusion that they should believe a lie, that they all might be damned, who believed not the truth, but had pleasure in unrighteousness' (*2 Thess.* 2:10–12). And what can such an one say for himself in the judgment, that shall be charged with the *abuse of love*? Christians, deny yourselves, deny your lusts, deny the vanities of this present life, devote yourselves to God; become lovers of God, lovers of his ways, and 'a people zealous of good works;' then shall you show one to another, and to all men, that you have not received the grace of God in vain (*2 Cor.* 6:1). Renounce therefore the hidden things of dishonesty, walk not in craftiness, nor handle God's word deceitfully, but by manifestation of the truth, commend yourselves to every man's conscience in the sight of God. Do this, I say, yea, and *so* endeavour such a closure with this love of God in Christ, as may graciously constrain you to do it, because, when all proofs of the right receiving of this love of Christ shall be produced, none will be found of worth enough to justify the simplicity of our profession, but that which makes us 'zealous of good works' (*Titus* 2:14). And what a thing will it be to be turned off at last, as one that abused the love of Christ! as one that presumed upon his lusts, this world, and all manner of naughtiness, because the love of Christ to pardon sins was so great! What an unthinking, what a disingenuous one wilt thou be counted at that day! yea, thou wilt be found to be the man that made a *prey* of love, that made a stalking-horse of love, that made of love a slave to sin, the devil and the world, and will not that be bad? Read Ezekiel 16.

iv) To use it to counter the weakness of faith.
Is the love of God and of Christ so great? let us then labour to improve it to the utmost for our advantage, against all the hindrances of faith.

To what purpose else is it revealed, made mention of, and commended to us? We are environed with many enemies, and faith in the love of God and of Christ, is our only succour and shelter. Wherefore our duty and wisdom and privilege is, to improve this love for our own advantage. Improve it against daily infirmities, improve it against the wiles of the devil; improve it against the threats, rage, death, and destruction, that the men of this world continually with their terror set before you. But how must that be done? why, set this love and the safety that is in it, before thine eyes; and behold it while these things make their assaults upon thee. These words, the faith of this, *God loves me*, will support thee in the midst of what dangers may assault thee. And this is that which is meant, when we are exhorted to rejoice in the Lord (*Phil.* 3:1); to make our boast in the Lord (*Psa.* 44:51); to triumph in Christ (*2 Cor.* 2:14); and to set the Lord always before our face (*Psa.* 16:8). For he that can do this thing stedfastly, cannot be overcome. For in God there is more than can be in the world, either to help or hinder; wherefore if God be my helper, if God loves me, if Christ be my redeemer, and has bestowed his love that passeth knowledge upon me, who can be against me? (*Heb.* 13:6; *Rom.* 8:31) and if they be against me, what disadvantage reap I thereby; since even all this also, worketh for my good? This is improving the love of God and of Christ for my advantage.

The same course should Christians also take with the degrees of this love, even set it against all the degrees of danger; for here *deep calleth unto deep*. There cannot be wickedness and rage wrought up to such or such a degree, as of which it may be said, there are not degrees in the love of God and of Christ to match it. Wherein Pharaoh dealt proudly against God's people, the Lord was above him (*Exod.* 18:11), did match and overmatch him; he came up to him, and went beyond him; he collared with him, overcame him, and cast him down. 'The Lord is a man of war, the Lord is his name. Pharaoh's chariots and the host hath he cast into the sea . . . and they sank into the bottom as a stone' (*Exod.* 15:5). There is no striving against the Lord that hath loved us; there is none that strive against him can prosper. If the shields of the earth be the Lord's (*Psa.* 47:9), then he can wield them for the safeguard of his body the church; or if they are become incapable of being made use of any longer in that way, and for such a thing, can he not lay them aside, and make himself new ones? Men can do after this manner, much more God. But again, if the miseries, or afflictions which thou meetest with, seem to thee to overflow, and to go beyond measure, above measure, and so to be above strength, and begin to drive thee to despair of life (*2 Cor.* 1:8); then thou hast also, in the love of God, and of Christ, that which is above, and that goes beyond all measure also, to wit, love unsearchable, unknown, and 'that can do exceeding abundantly above all that we ask or think.' Now God hath set them one against the other, and 'twill be thy wisdom to do so too, for this is the way to improve this love. But, though it be easy, thus to admonish you to do, yet you shall find the practical part more difficult; wherefore, here it may not be amiss, if I add to these, another head of COUNSEL.

(2) WAYS TO DO THIS

i) Strive to find and feel it

Then, Wouldst thou *improve* this love of God and of Christ to thy advantage, Why then *thou must labour after the knowledge of it*. This was it that the Apostle prayed for, for these Ephesians, as was said before, and this is that that thou must labour after, or else thy *reading* and my *writing*, will, as to thee, be fruitless. Let me then say to thee, as David to his son Solomon, 'And thou Solomon, my son, know thou the God of thy father' (*1 Chron.* 28:9). Empty *notions* of this love will do nothing but harm, wherefore, they are not empty notions that I press thee to rest in, but that thou labour after the knowledge of the Savour of this good ointment (*Song of Sol.* 1:3), which the Apostle calleth the Savour of the knowledge of this Lord Jesus (*2 Cor.* 2:14). Know it, until it becometh *sweet* or pleasant to thy soul, and then it will *preserve* and keep thee (*Prov.* 2:10, 11). Make this love of God and of Christ *thine own*, and not another's. Many there are that can talk largely of the love of God to Abraham, to David, to Peter and Paul. But that is not the thing, give not over until this love be made thine own; until thou *find* and *feel* it to run warm in thy heart by the shedding of it abroad there, by the spirit that God hath given thee (*Rom.* 5:5). Then thou wilt know it with an obliging and engaging knowledge; yea, then thou wilt know it with a soul-strengthening, and soul-encouraging knowledge.

ii) Set it in opposition to the love of all others things.

Wouldst thou improve this love? then set it against the love of all other things whatsoever, even until this love shall conquer thy soul from the love of them to itself.

This is Christian. Do it therefore, and say, why should any thing have my heart but God, but Christ? He loves me, he loves me with love that passeth knowledge. He loves me, and he shall have me: he loves me, and I will love him: his love stripped him of all for my sake; Lord let my love strip me of all for thy sake. I am a son of love, an object of love, a monument of love, of *free* love, of *distinguishing* love, of *peculiar* love, and of love that passeth knowledge: and why should not I walk in love? In love to God, in love to men, in holy love, in love unfeigned? This is the way to improve the love of God for thy advantage, for the subduing of thy passions, and for sanctifying of thy nature. 'Tis an odious thing to hear men of base lives talking of the love of God, of the death of Christ, and of the glorious grace that is presented unto sinners by the word of the truth of the gospel. Praise is comely for the upright, not for the profane. Therefore let him speak of love that is *taken* with love, that is *captivated* with love, that is *carried away* with love. If this man speaks of it, his speaking signifies something; the powers, and bands of love are upon him, and he shows to all that he knows what he is speaking of. But the very mentioning of love, is in the mouth of the profane, like a parable in the mouth of fools, or as salt unsavory. Wherefore, Christian, improve this love of God as thou *shouldest*, and that will improve thee as thou *wouldest*. Wherefore,

iii) *Keep oneself in it*

If thou wouldest improve this love, keep thyself in it. 'Keep yourselves in the love of God' (*Jude* 21). This text looks as if it favoured the Socinians, but there is nothing of that in it. And so doth that, 'If ye keep my commandments, ye shall bide in my love: even as I have kept my Father's commandments and abide in his love' (*John* 15:10). The meaning then is this, that living a holy life is the way, after a man has believed unto justification, to keep himself in the savour and comfort of the love of God. And Oh, that thou wouldest indeed so do. And that because, if thou shall want the savour of it, thou will soon want tenderness to the commandment, which is the rule by which thou must walk, if thou wilt do good to thyself, or honour God in the world. 'To him that ordereth *his* conversation *aright*, will I shew the salvation of God' (*Psa.* 50:23). He that would live a sweet, comfortable, joyful life, must live a very holy life. This is the way to improve this love to thyself indeed.

iv) *Be established in the doctrine and basis of it*

To this end, you must take root and be grounded in love; that is, you must be well settled, and stablished in this love, if indeed you would improve it. You must not be shaken as to the doctrine and grounds of it (*Eph.* 3:17). These you must be well acquainted with: for he that is but a child in this doctrine, is not capable as yet, of falling in with these exhortations: For such waver and fear when tempted; and 'he that feareth is not made perfect in love' (*1 John* 4:18), nor can he so improve it for himself and soul's good as he should.

v) *Be assured of its comforts already enjoyed*

And lastly, Keep, to this end, those grounds, and evidences that God hath given you of your call to be partakers of this love, with all clearness upon your hearts, and in your minds. For he that wants a sight of them, or a proof that they are true and good, can take but little comfort in this love. There is a great mystery in the way of God with his people. He will justify them without their works, he will pardon them for his Son's sake: but they shall have but little comfort of what he hath done, doth, and will do for them that are careless, carnal, and not holy in their lives. Nor shall they have their evidences for heaven at hand, nor out of doubt with them, yea, they shall walk without the sun, and have their comforts by bits and knocks;* while others sit at their father's table, have liberty to go into the wine-cellar, rejoice at the sweet and pleasant face of their heavenly Father towards them; and know it shall go well with them at the end.

---

* 'Bits and knocks'; this phrase is now obsolete: it alludes to a dog at table, who while picking up the crumbs, often gets a bite and a knock with it, but still perseveres.—Ed.

3: The Message of this Good Will to Unbelievers

Something now for a conclusion should be spoken to the carnal world, who have heard me tell of all this love. But what shall I say unto them? If I should speak to them, and they should not hear; or if I should testify unto them, and they should not believe; or intreat them, and they should scorn me; all will but aggravate, and worsen their sin, and tend to their further condemnation. And therefore I shall leave the obstinate where I found him, and shall say to him that is willing to be saved, Sinner, thou hast the advantage of thy neighbour, not only because thou art willing to live, but because there are [those] that are willing thou shouldest; to wit, those unto whom the issues from death do belong, and they are the Father and the Son, to whom be glory with the blessed Spirit of grace, world without end. Amen.

ANALYSIS OF TREATISE

PART ONE
DESCRIBING THE INEXPRESSIBLE

1 *Ephesians 3:18, 19 in Context*
    (i) The terms of measurement
    (ii) The reason for their use
    (iii) The fulness implied in them

2 *The Breadth of Christ's Love*

3 *The Length of Christ's Love*

4 *The Depth of Christ's Love*

5 *The Height of Christ's Love*

PART TWO
DESIRING THE INCOMPARABLE

1 *Praying For An Ability*

2 *Praying For An Understanding*
    (i) a mark of the gospel minister
    (ii) an indication of benefits available which are:
        a) a sense of God's greatness
        b) a confidence before the world
        c) a reverence before God
        d) a willingness that he should be our God
        e) a better grasp of the glory to come
        f) a sure conviction of the end of all things
        g) a greater longing for heaven

3 *Praying For A Knowledge*
  (i) Of the love of Christ
      a) Who Christ is
      b) What love is
      c) What the love of Christ is which is made
         known by:
          (i) his actual dying
          (ii) his preparations for dying
          (iii) his achievements through death which
               are that:
               a) he has reconciled every one of the elect
               b) he has destroyed all their infernal
                  foes
               c) he has obtained the Holy Spirit
                  for his people
               d) he has become Lord of all for them
               e) he has given gifted ministers to
                  his church
               f) he has occupied heaven for his own
  (ii) Of its unsearchableness
       because it surpasses the knowledge of
      a) the wisest saint
      b) all the saints
      c) the saints in heaven
      d) all the redeemed and all the angels in heaven
         because
          (i) it is eternal, infinite and incomprehen-
              sible and to know it fully means that we
              must fully know:
          (ii) all sin's nature, aggravations and
               tendencies
          (iii) all the wiles and opposition of the
                devil
          (iv) all that Christ has procured by his blood

PART THREE

OBTAINING THE UNSURPASSABLE

Christ's love can be known

1 In its nature which is free, divine, heavenly, everlasting and incorruptible.

Helps to knowing this

(i) Know oneself as a sinner

(ii) Strive to know the poverty and pollution of human righteousness

(iii) Become familiar with the nature of the law and the nature of the gospel

(iv) Keep each of these in its proper place

2 In many of its degrees

(i) By contemplating his incarnation in which:

a) he united our nature to God

b) he was made our representative

c) he defeated our foes and made us conquerors

d) he occupied heaven for us as a forerunner

e) he sent the Holy Spirit to be a comforter

f) he sympathises with his people though he is in heaven

g) he intercedes for them

h) he will bring us where he is

(ii) By pondering the fact that he passed by fallen angels to save us even though:

a) he would not have needed to stoop so low to save angels as humans

b) they probably would have recognised him and responded better than we

c) had God chosen them, we would not have been able to hinder their faith and hope, as they do ours

remaining sin more easily than we

   e) they would probably have kept the law more fully and promptly

   f) they would have praised God more worthily than we

  (iii) By pondering the effort involved to bring sinners to glory

    a) they are an enemy against him

    b) they are averse to being taught by him

    c) they are prone to wander from him

    d) they sin openly and refuse to confess it

    e) he chastises them instead of destroying them

    f) he preserves his work in their hearts

    g) he loves them more and more

    h) he delights most in loving the worst

3 In knowing it as something that is beyond knowing
  This is shown by:

  (i) The statement in the text itself

  (ii) The examples of great men of God

  (iii) The advantages of knowing in part which are

    a) It is a means of recovery from a time of temptation

    b) It is a resource for Christian living in a time of difficulty

    c) It promotes a desire to press forward to glory

    d) It leads to being 'filled with the fulness of God'

PART FOUR

USES AND COUNSELS

(I) See the greatness of God's good will to believers!

(II) It calls believers:
- (i) to ponder and search after it
- (ii) to cast themselves on it
- (iii) to take heed of abusing it
- (iv) to use it to counter the weakness of faith

(III) Ways to do this
- (i) Strive to find and feel it
- (ii) Set it in opposition to the love of all things
- (iii) Keep oneself in it
- (iv) Be established in the doctrine and basis of it
- (v) Be assured of its comforts already enjoyed

(IV) It assures unbelievers that if any are willing to believe and live, the Father, Son and Spirit are willing too.